OFFICIAL STRATEGY GUIDE

DESCENT: FREESPACE
THE GREAT WAR

BY MARK H. WALKER

LEGAL STUFF

Brady Publishing
An Imprint of Macmillan Digital Publishing USA
201 W. 103rd Street
Indianapolis, Indiana 46290

ISBN: 1-56686-787-8

Library of Congress Catalog No.: 98-070850

Printing Code: The rightmost double-digit number is the year of the book's printing; the rightmost single-digit number is the number of the book's printing. For example, 98-1 shows that the first printing of the book occurred in 1998.

00 99 98   3 2 1

Manufactured in the United States of America.

BradyGAMES Staff

Publisher
Lynn Zingraf

Editor-In-Chief
H. Leigh Davis

Title/Licensing Manager
David Waybright

Marketing Manager
Janet Cadoff

Acquisitions Editor
Debra McBride

Credits

Development Editor
David Cassady

Project Editor
Timothy Fitzpatrick

Technical Editor
Henly Wolin

Screenshot Editor
Michael Owen

Creative Director/Book Designer
Scott Watanabe

Production Designer
Jane Washburne

About the Author

Mark H. Walker is a former Naval Officer and Explosive Ordnance Disposal diver. He has been writing professionally for seven years. During that time, he has written numerous magazine articles on computer technology, computer gaming, and auto racing for major publications, such as *Autoweek*, *Playboy*, *Computer Gaming World*, *Computer Games Strategy Plus*, and *Sierra Interaction*. Additionally, he has authored eight books, including *How to Use the Internet*, and gaming strategy guides on *Nascar Racing 2*, *SODA Off-Road Racing*, *ABC Sports Indy Racing*, *Warcraft II*, *Magic: the Gathering—Battlemage*, and *Diablo: Battle.net*.

Mark recently escaped from hectic city life and resides in rural Virginia. He now lives ten miles from the closest fast food restaurant with his wife Janice, and their three daughters: Denver, Jessica, and Ayron.

Author Acknowledgments

Thanks to: Debra McBride for the work, John Elway for the heart, Natalie Imbruglia for the voice, Mike Emberson for the help, my wife for the love, my daughters for the inspirations, and Jerry Seinfeld for the laughs.

Mark H. Walker
Author: Technical Journals, Computer Game Strategy Guides,
Fiction 9563 Henry Road Henry, VA 24102
www.markhwalker.com
mwalker@neocomm.net
(540) 629-2917

TABLE OF CONTENTS

INTRODUCTION

INTRODUCTION

A wise man said that only two things are certain in life: death and taxes. Unfortunately, this wise man, whoever he was, never met a science fiction buff. If so, he would've surely added a third thing to his list: battling hostile alien forces who are trying to conquer the universe. Every sci-fi junkie knows this—heck, even expects it.

From H.G. Wells' *War of the Worlds* to George Lucas' *Star Wars*, the heavens are populated with battles galore. And in the realm of sci-fi gaming, war is essentially a way of life, the final round of biological evolution set in that gigantic boxing ring we call the universe.

The object of this cosmic fistfight is simple. One species, or a confederation of several species, is vying for the galactic head honcho title. In the macrocosm the game gods have envisioned for us, victory is the only option and survival the bottom-line.

Interplay's *Descent: FreeSpace: The Great War* is no exception to this space-opera formula. Our human progeny, under the banner of the Galactic Terran Alliance (GTA), are trying to keep peace with their neighbors, or at least share the head honcho title. But first, their old adversaries—the Vasudans—and later, their spanking new adversaries—the Shivans—try to crash the party. Both alien species want total galactic domination, and a war of titanic proportion ensues.

ENOUGH HISTORY, HOW DOES IT PLAY?

That's fine, but what about the game? After all, gamers don't want to pretend they're in some distant corner of the universe, they want to *be* there. They want that—to use the current industry buzzword— immersion experience.

Well, if you want immersion, you came to the right piece of software. From the Shivan's blood-red lasers to the howl of wide open GTA fighters, this game sucks you out of your chair and tosses you into the vacuum of space a billion light years away.

But smoking unfriendly alien life forms is only part of the thrill. A rich history and a deep plot put you in your pilot's boots and make you want to blast the enemy, be it Vasudan or Shivan.

In short, *Descent: FreeSpace* is a mind-blowing experience. Science fiction has never appeared so, yes I'm gonna say it, *real*. But if you *really* want to win, you'll need a little help, and that's where we come in. Follow along and you'll be turning Scorpions into metal shards before you know it.

The Book

If you want to save the world, you had better know how to do it. This book will show you how. As your official strategy guide, you will find enough tactics, tips, and background information here to keep you on course to cosmic victory.

But before you take off, let me give you some advice. There are two ways to use a strategy guide. One, you can read it from cover to cover. This is what I recommend. However, not everyone has time to read a whole book. After all, reality often interferes with gaming lives. For those of you who don't have access to a time machine or the subspace technology of the GTA, the Vasudans, and the Shivans, you may choose to just scan the sections that interest you. That's all right; you'll still pick up what you need, and it's for your lifestyle that the following synopsis of the book's chapters is listed.

The Introduction

This, of course, is what you're reading now, just a briefing on the game and the layout of the book.

CHAPTER 1:
THE GALACTIC TERRAN ALLIANCE (GTA)
SPACECRAFT

For starters, learn whom the good guys and gals are. This section contains vital information on the spacecraft that you will man against the aliens. It's all here, from data to illustrations.

CHAPTER 2:
THE VASUDAN SPACECRAFT

A rundown on the guys who the GTA has had its hands full with for the past 14 years. Get the new and improved scouting report.

CHAPTER 3:
THE SHIVAN
SPACECRAFT

Meet your new enemies. The Shivans are the embodiment of destruction, the wrecking ball that is smashing up civilizations, both that of the GTA and the Vasudans. Included is raw data, background, and screenshots on this race that has a gut-wrenching penchant for wiping out history.

CHAPTER 4:
THE WALK-ONS

Got questions about such things as miscellaneous craft, mines, and containers? This section has the answers.

CHAPTER 5:
THE WEAPONS OF DESCENT: FREESPACE

If you think that a Tsunami is just a large tidal wave in the ocean, or that a stiletto is some type of dagger, you definitely need to read this section. Interplanetary warfare has gone high-tech!

CHAPTER 6:
GENERAL PILOTING STRATEGIES

This chapter offers some general piloting strategies for all you future Luke Skywalkers and Captain Kirks out there.

CHAPTERS 7-9:
THE MISSIONS

Descent: FreeSpace contains many missions. Each campaign is split into three acts. This book covers an act in each chapter. This is the place to find the banking turn, pitching dive, and blasting laser account of how to win each mission, impress your friends, woo the significant other of your dreams, and move on to fame and stardom. Okay, I'm kidding about the fame and stardom.

CHAPTER 10:
MULTIPLAYER MISSIONS

Ah, lasing your hunk of silicon, plastic, and wires is fun. But it's nothing compared to putting a MX-50 up your boss' butt. This chapter shows you how to beat the supreme enemy—another human—as this chapter walks through each of *Descent: FreeSpace's* multiplayer missions.

The End of The Beginning

That's it. I've told you what I'm going to tell you. Now, don your pilot's helmet and go learn it firsthand.

GTA SPACECRAFT

Chapter One:
The Galactic Terran Alliance(The Good Guys)

Welcome, cadets, to *Descent: FreeSpace* 101. Contained in this manual is everything you need to know to defeat Terra's enemies. It's crunch time, boys and girls, so hop on aboard and take a look at the arsenal you'll use to save the universe.

The Statistics

Following is a list of the terms used to describe the capabilities of Terran ships. You'll need to understand the meanings of these terms, as knowing the relative strengths and weaknesses of the tools at your disposal will enable you to strategize wisely.

Maximum Velocity: *Top speed in meters per second.*

Acceleration Factor: *A measurement of how quickly the ship accelerates. The higher the number, the more slowly the ship accelerates.*

Deceleration Factor: *A measurement of how quickly the ship decelerates. The higher the number, the more slowly the ship decelerates.*

Permissable Gun Systems: *The types of guns allowed on the ship.*

Default Gun Systems: *Types of guns that are standard issue for each ship.*

Permissable Missles: *The missiles that are allowed on ship.*

Default Missles: *The types of missiles the ship is usually equipped with.*

Shields: *The power of the ship's shields. The higher the number, the better.*

Power Output: *The energy output (per second) of the ship's reactor.*

Afterburner: *Does the ship have an afterburner? (YES or NO)*

Afterburner Max Velocity: *Speed of ship with afterburner engaged.*

Fighters

Like many of the mythological beings they are named after, these "children of the imagination" are out of this world. Each type of vessel is different. Learn which is right for your mission. This is the critical lesson here. Better to learn now, in the quiet of your reading chair, than later, while being bombarded by Shivan firepower.

GTF Ulysses

The GTF Ulysses is the joint brainchild of Terran and Vasudan cooperation. Generally speaking, it is your best bet in space due to its power and maneuverability. A word of caution to you trigger-happy pilots out there: what Ulysses has in speed, it lacks in firepower.

Maximum Velocity:	70
Acceleration Factor:	2
Deceleration Factor:	1.5
Permissible Gun Systems:	ML-16 Laser, Disruptor, Flail, Prometheus, Avenger, D-Advanced
Default Gun Systems:	Avenger, ML-16 Laser
Permissible Missles:	MX-50, D-Missle, Hornet, Interceptor
Default Missles:	MX-50
Shields:	260
Power Output:	2
Afterburner:	YES
Afterburner Max Velocity:	150

GTF Apollo

Not only is the Apollo the first ship of Terran origin, but it is also the easiest to fly. Versatility is Apollo's forte, although it allows little choice in gun and laser weapon compliment.

Maximum Velocity:	60
Acceleration Factor:	3
Deceleration Factor:	1.5
Permissible Gun Systems:	ML-16 Laser, Disruptor, Flail, Avenger
Default Gun Systems:	Avenger, ML-16 Laser
Permissible Missiles:	MX-50, D-Missile, Fury, Interceptor, Hornet
Default Missiles:	MX-50, MX-50
Shields:	280
Power Output:	2
Afterburner:	YES
Afterburner Max Velocity:	140

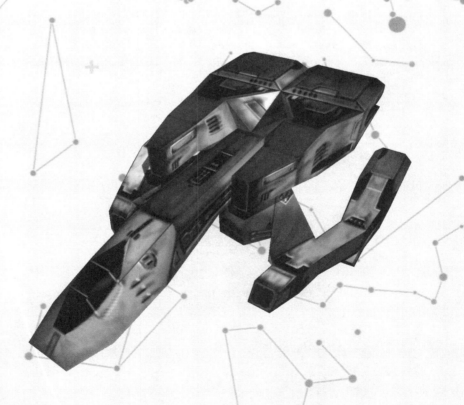

GTF Valkyrie

This is the ship to use when intercepting bombers. The Valkyrie has mind-blowin' speed and can carry any primary (gun and laser) weapon of your choice.

Maximum Velocity:	85
Acceleration Factor:	1
Deceleration Factor:	0.5
Permissible Gun Systems:	ML-16 Laser, Disruptor, Avenger, Prometheus, Banshee
Default Gun Systems:	ML-16 Laser, Prometheus
Permissible Missiles:	MX-50, D-Missile, Fury, Interceptor, Phoenix V, Hornet
Default Missiles:	MX-50
Shields:	300
Power Output:	2
Afterburner:	YES
Afterburner Max Velocity:	165

GTF Hercules

As you can guess, they don't call this daddy Hercules for nothing. It is the heavy assault fighter of the Terrans, with its nearly impenetrable hull and ability to harbor most weapons of choice. However, there is a downside to all its brute and size: compared to the other ships, Hercules provides little speed and a low level of maneuverability.

Maximum Velocity:	50
Acceleration Factor:	3
Deceleration Factor:	1.5
Permissible Gun Systems:	ML-16 Laser, Disruptor, Avenger, Flail, Prometheus, Banshee
Default Gun Systems:	Avenger, Disruptor
Permissible Missiles:	MX-50, D-Missile, Fury, Interceptor, Phoenix V, Hornet
Default Missiles:	Interceptor, Fury
Shields:	300
Power Output:	3
Afterburner:	YES
Afterburner Max Velocity:	120

BOMBERS

Bombers are the craft of choice for taking out large targets. Although they lack the maneuverability of most fighters, they pack one heck of a wallop.

GTB ATHENA

One of the earliest of Terran designs, the Athena is still in use today. Although it has an extremely vulnerable hull and a nearly obsolete storage capacity for the new weapons, it's still your best bet for a quick strike.

Maximum Velocity:	60
Acceleration Factor:	4
Deceleration Factor:	2
Permissible Gun Systems:	ML-16 Laser, Avenger, Flail, Disruptor
Default Gun Systems:	Avenger, Flail
Permissible Missiles:	D-Missile, Fury, Phoenix V, Synaptic, Stiletto
Default Missiles:	Phoenix V, Stiletto
Shields:	400
Power Output:	3
Afterburner:	Yes
Afterburner Max Velocity:	120

GTB Medusa

This craft is named after the snake-haired Gorgon who could turn men's faces to stone. This will surely be the case with your targeted capital ship opponents when they face a wing of Medusas. Enemy fighters, however, will easily waste your Medusas.

Maximum Velocity:	50
Acceleration Factor:	4
Deceleration Factor:	2
Permissible Gun Systems:	ML-16 Laser, Avenger, Prometheus
Default Gun Systems:	Avenger
Permissible Missiles:	MX-50, Hornet, Phoenix V, Stiletto, Synaptic, Tsunami
Default Missiles:	Hornet, MX-50, Tsunami
Shields:	600
Power Output:	4
Afterburner:	YES
Afterburner Max Velocity:	100

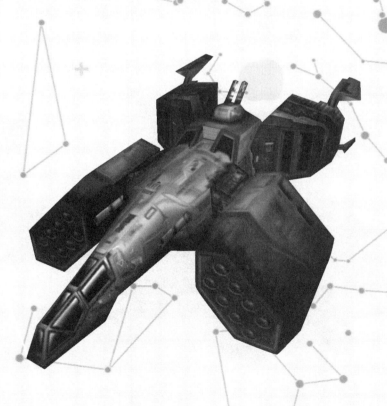

GTB Ursa

The Ursa is the GTA's biggest bomber. In fact, it's larger than all the fighters. Ursa is also the only Terran ship that can carry the feared Harbinger bomb. But before you get ready to hop into that cockpit, remember one thing: even though this ship has great armor and shields, it's wise to escort it with fighters.

Maximum Velocity:	45
Acceleration Factor:	4
Deceleration Factor:	2
Permissible Gun Systems:	ML-16 Laser, Disruptor, Avenger, Flail, Prometheus
Default Gun Systems:	Avenger, Avenger
Permissible Missiles:	MX-50, D-Missile, Fury, Interceptor, Hornet, Phoenix V, Synaptic, Stiletto, Tsunami
Default Missiles:	MX-50, Synaptic, Tsunami
Shields:	800
Power Output:	4.5
Afterburner:	YES
Afterburner Max Velocity:	90

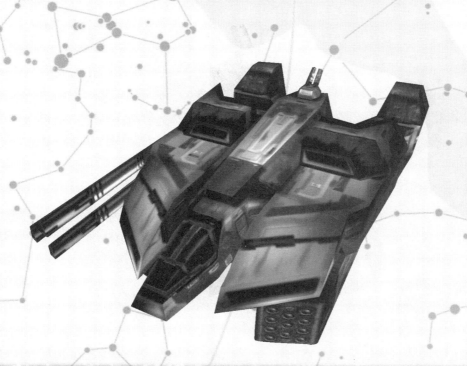

Non-Pilotable Craft

No, you can't jump onto the bridge of a Fenris class cruiser, but it's still nice to know its capabilities.

GTFR Poseidon

This craft is the most powerful of all the Terran freighters. However, as a ship, its armored plating is very weak and is only made more vulnerable by a total absence of shields.

Maximum Velocity:	50
Acceleration Factor:	4
Deceleration Factor:	1
Default Gun Systems:	4 Avenger Turrets
Default Missile Systems:	None
Shields:	0
Power Output:	30
Afterburner:	NO
Afterburner Max Velocity:	0

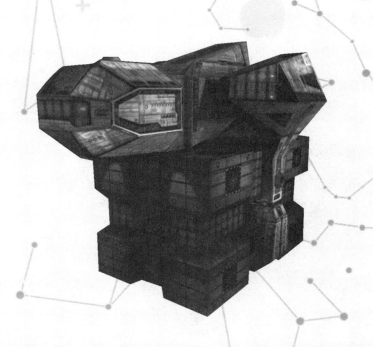

GTFR Chronos

Unlike the Poseidon, this freighter was designed for civilian use only. Its sole purpose lies in hauling cargo. Although Chronos is slow, it has an almost indestructible hull.

Maximum Velocity:	40
Acceleration Factor:	5
Deceleration Factor:	1.5
Default Gun Systems:	1 Avenger Turret
Default Missile Systems:	None
Shields:	0
Power Output:	1
Afterburner:	NO
Afterburner Max Velocity:	0

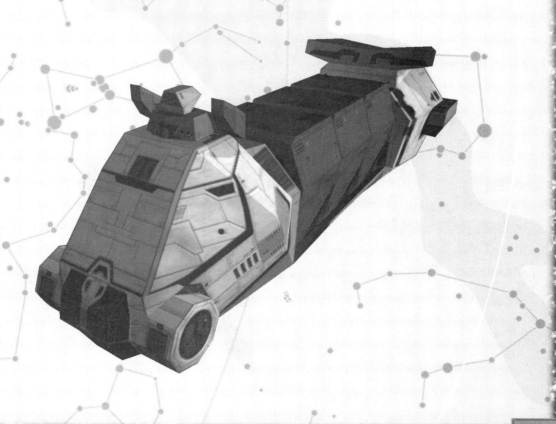

GTC Fenris

The first of the Terran cruiser fleet, Fenris has both defensive and strike capabilities. What it lacks in speed, it has in armor.

Maximum Velocity:	*20*
Acceleration Factor:	*10*
Deceleration Factor:	*5*
Default Gun Systems:	*8 Laser Turrets, 1 Fusion Mortar*
Default Missile Systems:	*None*
Shields:	*0*
Power Output:	*90*
Afterburner:	*NO*
Afterburner Max Velocity:	*0*

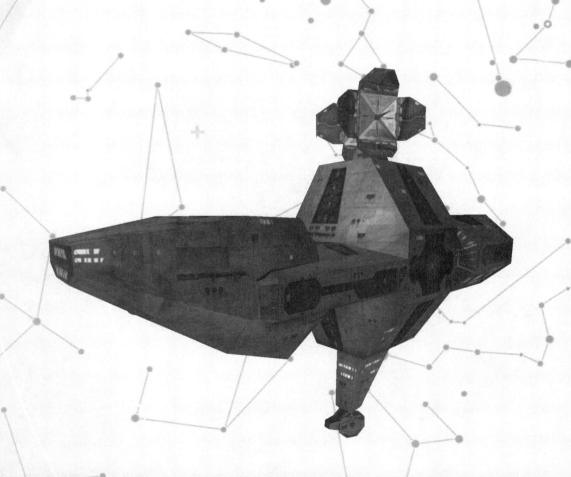

THE GALACTIC TERRAN ALLIANCE
(THE GOOD GUYS)

GTC LEVIATHAN

Meet the other GTA cruiser, the Leviathan. Like the Fenris class cruisers, Leviathan has an almost impenetrable hull.

Maximum Velocity:	10
Acceleration Factor:	18
Deceleration Factor:	7
Default Gun Systems:	4 Laser Turrets, 4 Avenger Turrets, 1 Synaptic Turret.
Default Missile Systems:	None
Shields:	0
Power Output:	90
Afterburner:	NO
Afterburner Max Velocity:	0

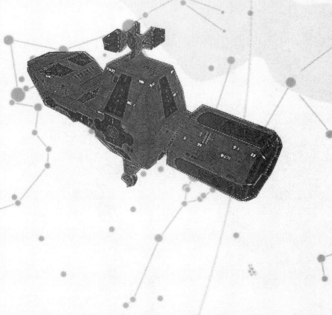

GTSC Faustus

The Faustus is a research vessel used both for civilian and military purposes. Due to this fact, enemy forces often try to seize or destroy these ships.

Maximum Velocity:	25
Acceleration Factor:	10
Deceleration Factor:	5
Default Gun Systems:	2 Light Laser Turrets, 1 Disruptor Turret, 3 ML-16 Laser Turrets,
Default Missile Systems:	1 Turret may have Fury or MX-50 missiles.
Shields:	0
Power Output:	20
Afterburner:	NO
Afterburner Max Velocity:	0

GTD Orion

Meet "Big Daddy." This is the largest and one of the most powerful of all Terran spacecraft. It is sure to leave all Vasudan and Shivan jaws dropped in awe. Note that the GTD Galatea and GTD Bastion are exact replicas of Orion (the only difference being the markings on the sides of the ships).

Maximum Velocity:	15
Acceleration Factor:	20
Deceleration Factor:	10
Default Gun Systems:	5 Triple Laser Turrets, 11 Laser Turrets.
Default Missile Systems:	None
Shields:	0
Power Output:	100
Afterburner:	NO
Afterburner Max Velocity:	0

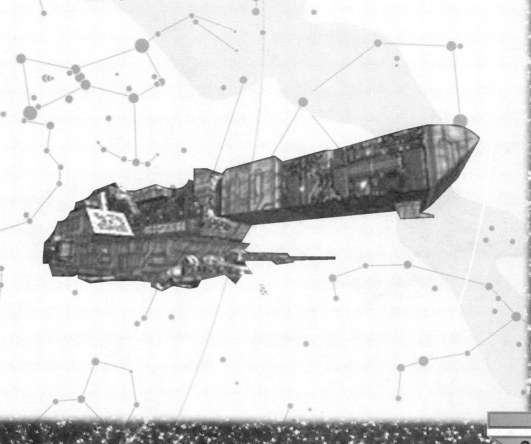

GTI Arcadia

Similar in concept to our space stations, Arcadian Installation Stations are used for a multitude of things. They are primarily trade and communication centers, but they also serve as ports and "repair shops" as well.

Maximum Velocity:	*0*
Acceleration Factor:	*0*
Deceleration Factor:	*0*
Default Gun Systems:	*11 Laser Turrets,*
Default Missile Systems:	*5 "Fighter Killer" missile batteries*
Shields:	*0*
Power Output:	*1*
Afterburner:	*NO*
Afterburner Max Velocity:	*0*

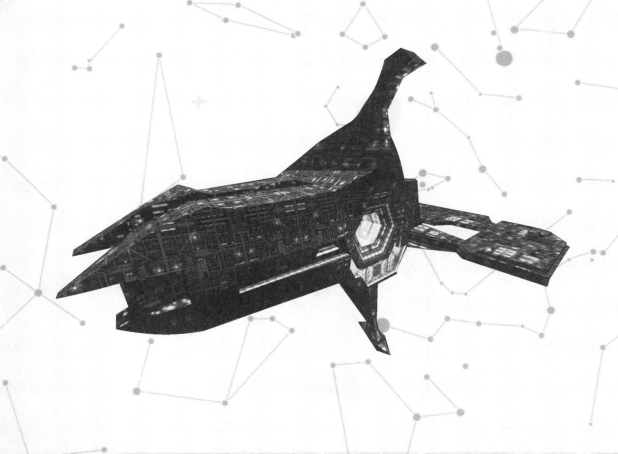

GTT Elysium

The GTT Elysium is a basic transport vessel. Its purpose is simple: to transport personnel and soldiers from place to place. Although she is very fast, she cannot take many hits. Elysium is one of those ships that will definitely need your protection.

Maximum Velocity:	40
Acceleration Factor:	6
Deceleration Factor:	1
Default Gun Systems:	1 ML-16 Laser Turret
Default Missile Systems:	None
Shields:	0
Power Output:	8
Afterburner:	NO
Afterburner Max Velocity:	0

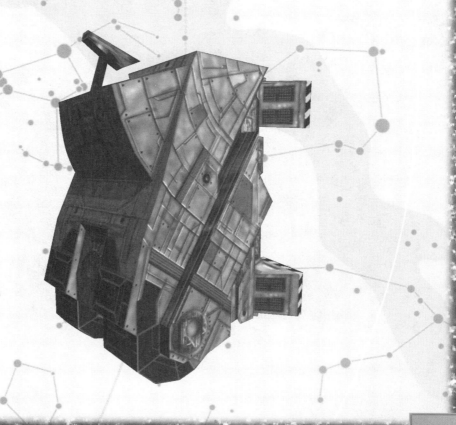

The End of Terra

Okay, that's it for the Terran systems. Now, let us review the enemy systems.

THE GALACTIC TERRAN ALLIANCE
(THE GOOD GUYS)

VASUDAN
SPACECRAFT

CHAPTER TWO:
THE VASUDANS
(THE BAD GUYS)

The Vasudans, the GTA's ex-enemies, aren't exactly anyone's idea of a good blind date. With their dry, leathery skin and two big eyes, they kinda remind people of mutant toads. Seriously, though, their physical appearance mirrors the planet they hail from. Vasuda Prime is basically a barren planet full of deserts and rocky mountains. The Vasudans have survived by looking for resources underground.

THE STATISTICS

Again, following, are quick descriptions regarding the terminology that you need to become familiar with in order to defend yourself adequately against Vasudan attack.

Maximum Velocity: *Top speed in meters per second.*

Acceleration Factor: *A measurement of how quickly the ship accelerates. The higher the number, the more slowly the ship accelerates.*

Deceleration Factor: *A measurement of how quickly the ship decelerates. The higher the number, the more slowly the ship decelerates.*

Default Gun Systems: *Types of guns that are standard issue for each ship.*

Default Missles: *The types of missiles the ship is usually equipped with.*

Shields: *The power of the ship's shields. The higher the number, the better.*

Power Output: *The energy output (per second) of the ship's reactor.*

Afterburner: *Does the ship have an afterburner? (YES or NO)*

Afterburner Max Velocity: *Speed of ship with afterburner engaged.*

FIGHTERS

Like their Terran counterparts, many of the ships are named by mythological references. Almost all Vasudan spacecraft, though, carry an Egyptian deity's namesake, an appropriate parallel between the desert dunes of Egypt and the scorched terrain of the planet Vasuda Prime. Also, like the GTA, the Vasudans have four prime fighters, each as versatile as yours. Prepare yourself—they're coming your way.

PVF ANUBIS

The Anubis is not fully loaded. The ship's arsenal is limited to the ML-16 Laser and Fury. But don't be fooled; with its speed and decent shield strength, this baby still has enough bite to get the job done.

Maximum Velocity:	*75*
Acceleration Factor:	*3*
Deceleration Factor:	*1.5*
Default Gun Systems:	*ML-16 Laser*
Default Missiles Systems:	*Fury*
Shields:	*200*
Power Output:	*2*
Afterburner:	*NO*
Afterburner Max Velocity:	*0*

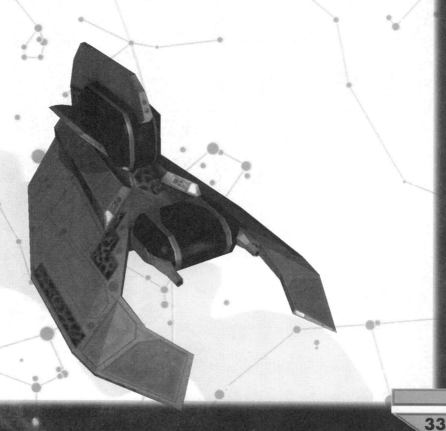

PVF Seth

Perhaps the most dangerous of all Vasudan fighters, the Seth gives the GTA Valkyrie a run for its money. It's equipped with lasers, guns, and missiles.

Maximum Velocity:	55
Acceleration Factor:	3
Deceleration Factor:	1.5
Default Gun Systems:	ML-16 Laser, Avenger
Default Missiles:	MX-50, Stiletto
Shields:	280
Power Output:	3
Afterburner:	YES
Afterburner Max Velocity:	130

PVF HORUS

If you feel the need for speed, you may want a piece of the Horus. This mama is the fastest known fighter to humankind—faster than those of the Terrans and Shivans. However, don't be too quick to hand out kudos to Vasudan engineering. The Horus has a major fault: she has the weakest shields of any fighter cruising the universe.

Maximum Velocity:	90
Acceleration Factor:	3
Deceleration Factor:	1.5
Default Gun Systems:	Avenger, Flail
Default Missiles:	MX-50, Phoenix V
Shields:	160
Power Output:	2
Afterburner:	YES
Afterburner Max Velocity:	170

PVF Thoth

Overall, the Thoth is an average fighter, but don't take it too lightly; it's equipped with one of most advanced laser systems, the Prometheus.

Maximum Velocity:	65
Acceleration Factor:	3
Deceleration Factor:	1.5
Default Gun Systems:	Prometheus
Default Missiles:	Interceptor
Shields:	200
Power Output:	2.5
Afterburner:	YES
Afterburner Max Velocity:	130

BOMBERS

Vasudan bombers are relatively weak. They are definitely not known for their speed, and their shield systems are weaker than those of their Terran and Shivan counterparts. I'd like to tell you that they're not a threat, but that depends on how you play your cards.

PVB OSIRIS

Osiris is a solid bomber. It's chief strength is that it carries the Phoenix V.

Maximum Velocity:	50
Acceleration Factor:	4
Deceleration Factor:	2
Default Gun Systems:	Avenger, 2 ML-16 Lasers
Default Missiles:	Synaptic, Stiletto, Phoenix V
Shields:	320
Power Output:	3
Afterburner:	YES
Afterburner Max Velocity:	100

PVB Amun

Another weak bomber, though not as weak as Osiris, Amun is loaded with a wider variety of weapons and is protected by a stronger shield system.

Maximum Velocity: 40
Acceleration Factor: 4
Deceleration Factor: 2
Default Gun Systems: Banshee, Avenger; 2 ML-16 Lasers in
                             subsystem
Default Missiles: Tsunami, Synaptic, Synaptic
Shields: 500
Power Output: 3.5
Afterburner: YES

Afterburner Max Velocity: 80

THE VASUDANS (THE BAD GUYS)

OTHER VASUDAN SPACE VESSELS

These primarily include freighters, with an occasional cruiser or destroyer in the picture. Vasudan space vessels are, relatively speaking, slow.

PVT Isis

The Isis is a transport vessel. It's smaller than the freighters, but effective in hauling light loads.

Maximum Velocity:	35
Acceleration Factor:	6
Deceleration Factor:	1
Gun Systems:	2 Avengers
Missiles Systems:	None
Shields:	0
Power Output:	2
Afterburner:	NO
Afterburner Max Velocity:	0

PVFR Bast

This is one big ship! What does that mean? She's an easy target—Bast has no shields and hardly any power.

Maximum Velocity:	50
Acceleration Factor:	5
Deceleration Factor:	1.5
Default Gun Systems:	Avenger, 2 Terran Turrets
Default Missiles Systems:	None
Shields:	0
Power Output:	1
Afterburner:	NO
Afterburner Max Velocity:	0

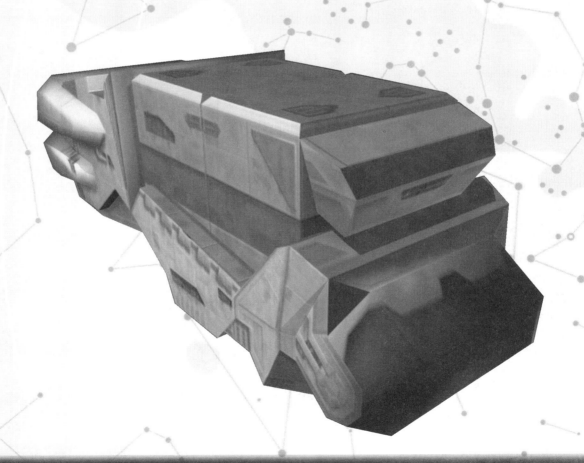

PVFR Ma'at

Ma'at is another easy target, very similar to the Bast. Feelin' lucky, cadets? Fire away!

Maximum Velocity:	50
Acceleration Factor:	7
Deceleration Factor:	1.5
Default Gun Systems:	Avenger, 2 Laser Turrets
Default Missile Systems:	None
Shields:	0
Power Output:	1
Afterburner:	NO
Afterburner Max Velocity:	0

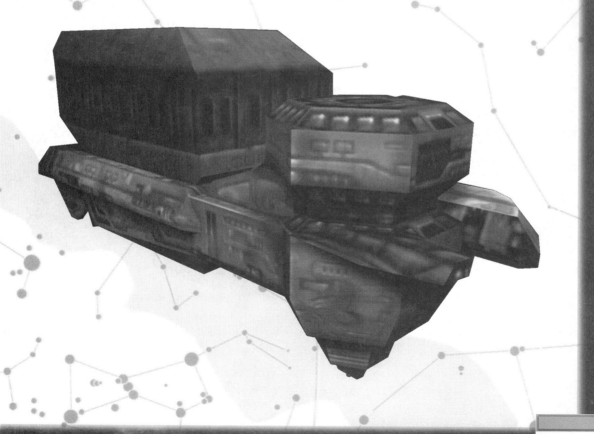

PVFR Satis

This is the only Vasudan freighter with shield protection. She'll be more of a challenge to destroy than the others.

Maximum Velocity:	50
Acceleration Factor:	7
Deceleration Factor:	4
Default Gun Systems:	5 Laser Turrets
Default Missile Systems:	None
Shields:	250
Power Output:	1
Afterburner:	NO
Afterburner Max Velocity:	0

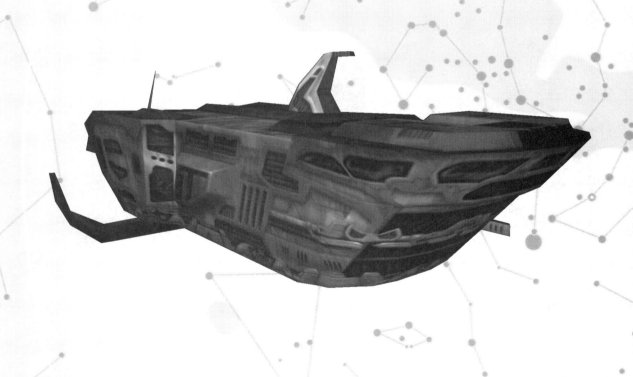

PVC ATEN

The Aten has one of the most powerful engines of all Vasudan space-craft. Although she is not lethally armed, she is equipped with six turrets.

Maximum Velocity:	25
Acceleration Factor:	10
Deceleration Factor:	5
Default Gun Systems:	2 Avengers, 4 Laser Turrets
Default Missile Systems:	None
Shields:	0
Power Output:	90
Afterburner:	NO
Afterburner Max Velocity:	0

PVD Typhon

An armed turtle, the Typhon is painfully slow, an easy target for GTA gun systems. But don't get too close and watch out while you're shooting—this baby is heavily armed.

Maximum Velocity:	*15*
Acceleration Factor:	*20*
Deceleration Factor:	*10*
Default Gun Systems:	*6 Laser Turrets, 2 Avengers, 5 Vasudan Flux Cannons*
Default Missile Systems:	*2 "Fighter Killer" Batteries*
Shields:	*0*
Power Output:	*100*
Afterburner:	*NO*
Afterburner Max Velocity:	*0*

That's all she wrote for our long-time enemies and new found allies. Now it's time to look at the *really* bad guys—the Shivans.

Shivan
Spacecraft

CHAPTER THREE:
THE SHIVANS
(THE REALLY BAD GUYS)

The Shivans are, simply put, a destructive juggernaut raging through the universe. Everything in their sight, whether Terran or Vasudan, is an object for siege. Spacecraft, installation stations, planets, and colonies all are targets for Shivan vessels.

The goal of these spider-like creatures appears to be nothing less than complete domination, and their methods seem to involve destroying both the human and Vasudan races. But some people believe the Shivans' motives are much more complex.

Since the discovery of an old manuscript from an extinct civilization called "the Ancients," new light has been shed on the Shivans. This document contains the only real information we have on this advanced species. In fact, what this manuscript turns up is quite puzzling. Some questions must be considered and understood if the GTA and the Vasudans plan on saving themselves from this new enemy.

What possible influence did the Shivans have upon our earthly ancestors? What is their worldview and purpose? And are they, in fact, as the "Hammer of Light" organization believes, the fulfillment of an ancient Vasudan prophecy?

THE STATISTICS

The following is listed again for your convenience. This time, of course, you will be focusing on the Shivan forces, learning as much as you can about their weapon systems.

Maximum Velocity: *Top speed in meters per second.*

Acceleration Factor: *A measurement of how quickly the ship accelerates. The higher the number, the more slowly the ship accelerates.*

Deceleration Factor: *A measurement of how quickly the ship decelerates. The higher the number, the more slowly the ship decelerates.*

Default Gun Systems: *Types of guns that are standard issue for each ship.*

Default Missles: *The types of missiles the ship is usually equipped with.*

Shields: *The power of the ship's shields. The higher the number, the better.*

Power Output: *The energy output (per second) of the ship's reactor.*

Afterburner: *Does the ship have an afterburner? (YES or NO)*

Afterburner Max Velocity: *Speed of ship with afterburner engaged.*

FIGHTERS

Most Shivan fighters are equipped with lasers of some sort but lack a large reserve of missiles. Overall, they are quicker than their Terran counterparts. However, the primary difference between their ships and ours lies in their shield system superiority.

SF DRAGON

One of the most powerful fighters of the fleet, the Dragon is a Shivan classic. She's armed with lasers and protected by an unbelievable range of shields.

Maximum Velocity:	*75*
Acceleration Factor:	*2*
Deceleration Factor:	*0.75*
Default Gun Systems:	*Shivan Heavy Laser, Shivan Heavy Laser*
Default Missiles:	*Interceptor*
Shields:	*700*
Power Output:	*2*
Afterburner:	*YES*
Afterburner Max Velocity:	*150*

SF Dragon #2

This is the weakest of the Dragons. It lacks the power that's present in the other models.

Maximum Velocity:	75
Acceleration Factor:	2
Deceleration Factor:	0.75
Default Gun Systems:	Shivan Heavy Laser, Shivan Heavy Laser
Default Missiles:	Fury
Shields:	700
Power Output:	0
Afterburner:	YES
Afterburner Max Velocity:	1

THE SHIVANS
(THE REALLY BAD GUYS)

SF Dragon #3

Armed and dangerous, this model is loaded with a wider array of gun systems and missiles than its two brothers are.

Maximum Velocity:	75
Acceleration Factor:	2
Deceleration Factor:	0.75
Permissible Gun Systems:	ML-16 Laser, Disruptor, Avenger, Flail, Prometheus, Banshee
Default Gun Systems:	Avenger, Prometheus
Permissible Missiles:	MX-50, D-Missile, Fury, Interceptor, Phoenix V, Hornet
Default Missiles:	Interceptor
Shields:	700
Power Output:	2
Afterburner:	YES
Afterburner Max Velocity:	90

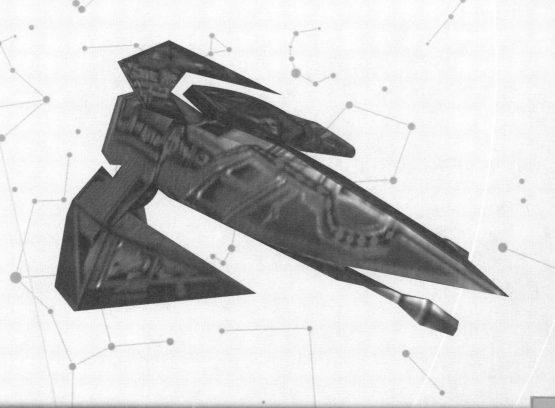

SF Basilisk

If you thought the Dragon fighters were bad news, you haven't seen the Basilisk yet. She has a similar arsenal, only a higher range of shield protection.

Maximum Velocity:	65
Acceleration Factor:	3
Deceleration Factor:	1.5
Default Gun Systems:	Shivan Mega Laser, Shivan Heavy Laser
Default Missiles:	Phoenix V, Hornet
Shields:	950
Power Output:	2.25
Afterburner:	YES
Afterburner Max Velocity:	110

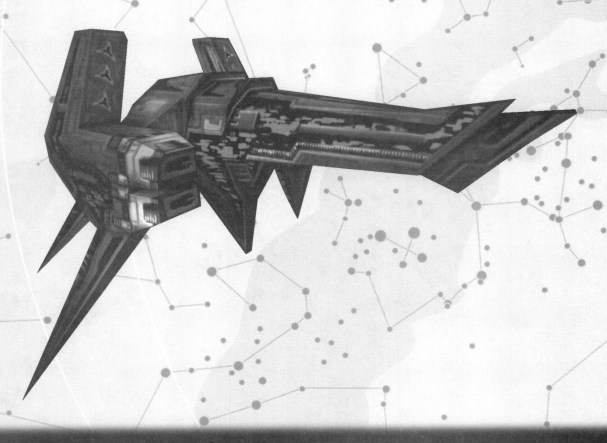

THE SHIVANS
(THE REALLY BAD GUYS)

SF Manticore

This model's primary claim to fame is its speed; it's the fastest of the Shivan fighters. However, lucky for us, the Manticore has the weakest shield protection of these fighters.

Maximum Velocity:	87
Acceleration Factor:	3
Deceleration Factor:	1.5
Default Gun Systems:	Shivan Mega Laser
Default Missiles:	Interceptor, MX-50
Shields:	500
Power Output:	1.5
Afterburner:	YES
Afterburner Max Velocity:	155

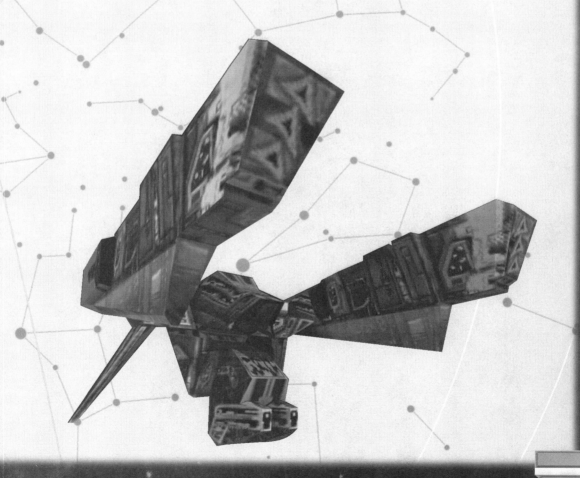

SF Scorpion

The baseline Shivan fighter, it is nothing special. Yet, beware; there is plenty of sting left in this Scorpion, and they come at you in swarms.

Maximum Velocity: 70
Acceleration Factor: 3
Deceleration Factor: 1.5
Default Gun Systems: Shivan Light Laser, Shivan Heavy Laser
Default Missiles: MX-50
Shields: 600
Power Output: 2
Afterburner: YES

Afterburner Max Velocity: 140

THE SHIVANS
(THE REALLY BAD GUYS)

BOMBERS

Terran bombers have an edge over the Shivans' in the weapons and afterburner departments, while they are both evenly matched in speed. The catch, however, is that Shivan bombers have over *twice* the shield strength of their GTA counterparts.

SB SHAITAN

This is the weaker of the two Shivan bombers. However, note that its shields are still more solid than any of those belonging to Terran bombers.

Maximum Velocity:	60
Acceleration Factor:	4
Deceleration Factor:	2
Default Gun Systems:	Shivan Light Laser, Shivan Heavy Laser
Default Missiles:	MX-50
Shields:	1000
Power Output:	3
Afterburner:	NO
Afterburner Max Velocity:	0

SB Nephilim

Not invincible, but effective, the Nephilim is equipped with everything necessary for a good hit-and-run strike. Watch out!

Maximum Velocity:	*60*
Acceleration Factor:	*4*
Deceleration Factor:	*2*
Default Gun Systems:	*Shivan Light Laser*
Default Missiles:	*MX-50, Synaptic, Phoenix V, MX-50*
Shields:	*1600*
Power Output:	*4*
Afterburner:	*NO*
Afterburner Max Velocity:	*0*

THE SHIVANS
(THE REALLY BAD GUYS)

OTHER SHIVAN SPACECRAFT

ST AZRAEL

The Azrael is a rare Shivan transport vehicle, vulnerable to Terran and Vasudan attack. Unlike most Shivan spacecraft, she has no shields whatsoever.

Maximum Velocity: 55
Acceleration Factor: 6
Deceleration Factor: 1
Default Gun Systems: 3 Shivan Light Lasers
Default Missiles: None
Shields: 0
Power Output: 8
Afterburner: NO

Afterburner Max Velocity: 0

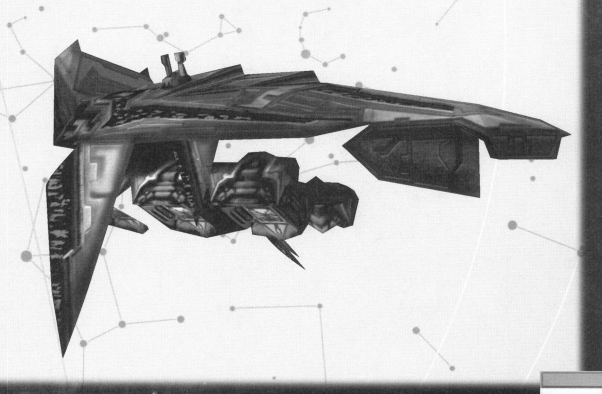

SFR Mephisto

In general, Shivan freighters, like the Mephisto, lack the thrust and power of the GTA line. Yet, this ship can still give Terran spacecraft a run for their money.

Maximum Velocity:	50
Acceleration Factor:	7
Deceleration Factor:	1.5
Default Gun Systems:	4 Shivan Light Lasers
Default Missiles:	None
Shields:	250
Power Output:	1
Afterburner:	NO
Afterburner Max Velocity:	0

SFR Asmodeus

The Asmodeus is one of the easiest targets in the Shivan fleet. Nevertheless, the Asmodeus' heavy laser is painful when it connects.

Afterburner:	NO
Afterburner Max Velocity:	50
Acceleration Factor:	7
Deceleration Factor:	1.5
Default Gun Systems:	Disruptor, Shivan Heavy Laser, 2 Shivan Light Lasers.
Permissible Missiles:	
Default Missiles:	
Shields:	0
Power Output:	1
Velocity:	0

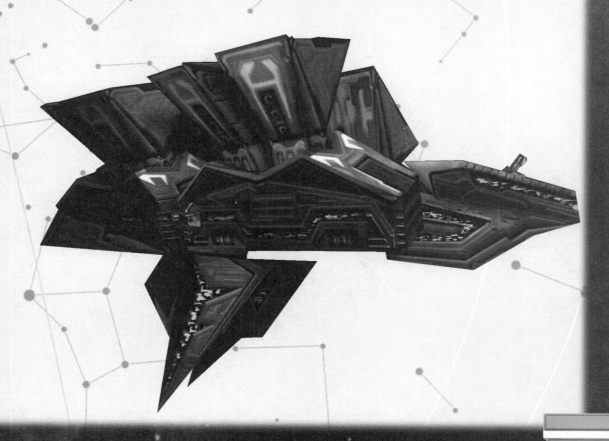

SC Lilith

If you wanted to create a cruiser with power, this would be it. Fortunately for you and the GTA, she is lacking in everything else.

Maximum Velocity:	*20*
Acceleration Factor:	*10*
Deceleration Factor:	*5*
Default Gun Systems:	*6 Shivan Turret Lasers, 1 Shivan Heavy Laser*
Default Missiles:	*2 Shivan Clusters*
Shields:	*0*
Power Output:	*90*
Afterburner:	*NO*
Afterburner Max Velocity:	*0*

THE SHIVANS
(THE REALLY BAD GUYS)

SC CAIN

This model is not just a cruiser, but a strike cruiser. Unlike the Lilith, it's quicker and contains a docking bay, but it has an extremely vulnerable hull.

Maximum Velocity:	30
Acceleration Factor:	10
Deceleration Factor:	10
Default Gun Systems:	4 Shivan Light Lasers, 3 Shivan Heavy Lasers
Default Missiles:	2 FighterKillers misslie batteries
Shields:	0
Power Output:	90
Afterburner:	NO
Afterburner Max Velocity:	0

SD DEMON

The Demon destroyer is very similar to its Terran counterparts, the Orion, the Galatea, and the Bastion. All of them are big, bad, and powerful.

Maximum Velocity:	*20*
Acceleration Factor:	*20*
Deceleration Factor:	*10*
Default Gun Systems:	*21 Shivan Lasers Turrets*
Default Missiles:	*4 FighterKillers missile bateries,*
	1 Swarmer battery
Shields:	*0*
Power Output:	*100*
Afterburner:	*NO*
Afterburner Max Velocity:	*0*

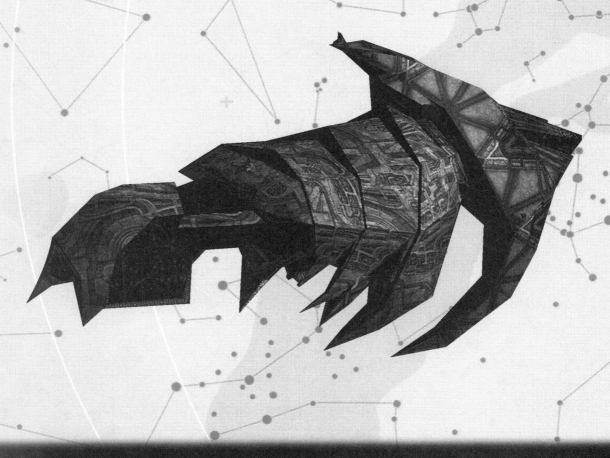

THE SHIVANS
(THE REALLY BAD GUYS)

SD Lucifer

A devil of a warship! Lucifer may be slow, but it has the strongest shields of any spacecraft in the universe, along with a heck of a subsystem load.

Maximum Velocity:	15
Acceleration Factor:	20
Deceleration Factor:	10
Default Gun Systems:	3 Super Shivan Lasers,
	12 Shivan Turret Lasers
Default Missiles:	1 Cluster, 1 Swarmer missile battery
Shields:	10,000
Power Output:	100
Afterburner:	NO
Afterburner Max Velocity:	0

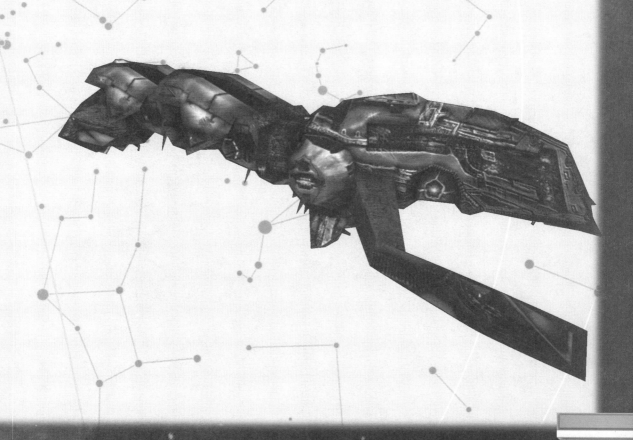

Well, that's it for the Shivans. Next up are the other things that float around in the freespace of Descent.

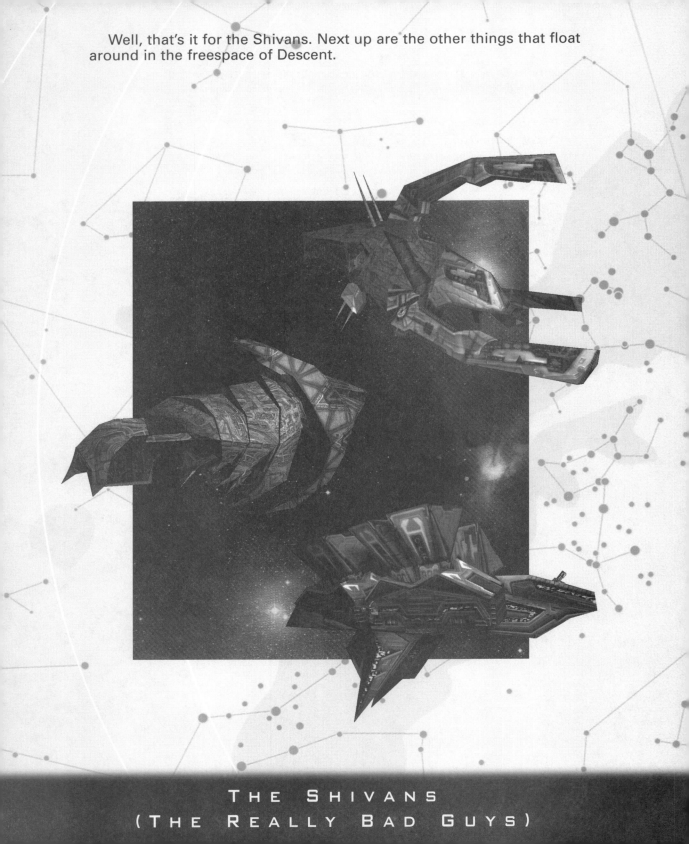

THE
WALK-ONS

Chapter 4: The Walk-Ons

This will be our fourth briefing before countdown, soldiers—and brief it will be. There are *ships* and there are *weapons*. In between these two are what I call the *walk-ons*. Walk-ons basically are just the couple or so odd items we find in the Descent universe. Although you won't see or use them often, they are out there. So, we'll answer your questions now to prevent later reports of UFOs.

Platform Sentry Guns

Used to defend bases and territory, the sentry gun is fielded by Terrans, Vasudans, and Shivans.

GTSG Watchdog

This baby is the most basic of Terran platform gun designs. Although effective, compared to the *Cerberus*, the *Watchdog* is just a puppy.

Hitpoints: 20

Default Weapons: 2 Laser Turrets

GTSG Cerberus

This Terran platform gun is named after the most famous sentry of all—the three-headed watchdog of hell, Cerberus. Guys (and gals), this dog is not just all bark, if you know what I mean. It's got the most "bite" of any platform weapon in the universe!

Hitpoints: 150

Default Weapons: 2 Avengers

PVSG Ankh

The *Ankh* is the Vasudans' primary sentry platform gun. It's the alien equivalent of the *GTSG Watchdog*.

Hitpoints: 20

Default Weapons: 2 Laser Turrets

SSG Trident

The second most powerful sentry gun in the known universe, this Shivan weapon is pure power. In fact, the *SSG Trident* has five times the power of the *Ankh* and the *Watchdog*.

Hitpoints: 100

Default Weapons: 2 Shivan Heavy Lasers

Escape Pods

Escape pods basically are your emergency ejection craft. They are not that fast and are very vulnerable to firepower. But hey, they are better than space's vacuum—at least for a crumbling starship's crew.

GTEP Hermes

This is your primary escape pod for Terran use. It's named after the messenger of the gods, the wing-footed Hermes.

Maximum Velocity: 40
Acceleration Factor: 2
Deceleration Factor: 1.5
Shields: 100

PVEP Ra

The Ra is the Vasudan escape pod. It is not very fast nor is it strong, so it should be an easy target for you Terran pilots. Don't let the enemy get away!

Maximum Velocity: 40
Shields: 100

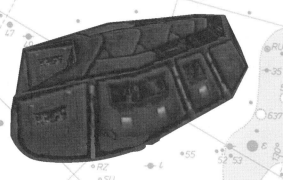

Miscellaneous

I know that most of what was mentioned previously was sort of...well, you know, miscellaneous, but here are just a few more things that you will find every now and then in the Descent universe.

Terran NavBuoy

These are guides to help you bring your ship in. There is no need to fire at these innocent guys, okay?

Hitpoints: 100

Asteroids

On some missions, you will need to navigate through some asteroids. You also can blow them out of the way with your guns. I recommend the latter.

Hitpoints: 100

Enough of this weak-kneed NavBuoy stuff. The next chapter looks at the "real-stuff" weapons.

THE TOOLS
OF WAR

CHAPTER 5:
THE TOOLS OF WAR—
WEAPONS OF
DESCENT: FREESPACE

Cruisers are awesome and Ulysses fighters are sexy, but weapons are the pointy end of combat's sword. Take a look at Descent: FreeSpace's dealers of punishment.

STATISTICS

I hope you still have an appetite for destruction, flyboys (and girls). You know the craft, now you need to know the weapons. The following is a listing of some key terms that you will need to adequately understand in order to help the Galactic Terran Alliance win this war.

Damage: *Estimated damage caused by each shot. The higher, the better.*

Rate of Fire: *Number of firings by weapon per second.*

Armor Damage Multiple: *A measure of the weapon's effectiveness against armor. The higher the better.*

Shield Damage Multiple: *A measure of the weapon's effectiveness against shields. The higher the better.*

Subsystem Damage Multiple: *A measure of the weapon's effectiveness against subsystems. The higher the better.*

Energy Consumed: *Amount of energy the weapon uses.*

PRIMARY WEAPONS

The primary weapons include projectile or energy-based gun systems of the GTA, Vasudans, and Shivans.

GTW ML-16 LASER

One of the GTA's favorite cannons for vaporizing an enemy ship's armor, the Laser can deliver substantial damage to the hull within a very short time.

Damage:	5
Rate of Fire:	5
Armor Damage Multiple:	1
Shield Damage Multiple:	0.1
Subsystem Damage Multiple:	0.3
Energy Consumed:	0.2

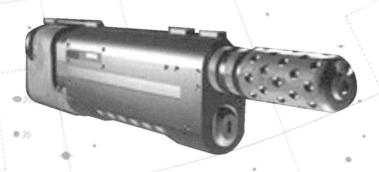

GTW-41 DISRUPTOR CANNON

The Disruptor is a gas-focused krypton laser used primarily for disabling enemy ship subsystems. It was designed specifically for tactical warfare.

Damage:	3.3
Rate of Fire:	15
Armor Damage Multiple:	0.5
Shield Damage Multiple:	0.1
Subsystem Damage Multiple:	1
Energy Consumed:	0.25

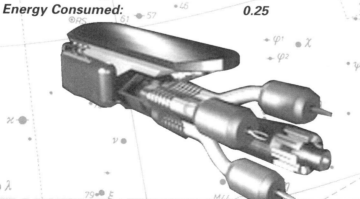

GTW-41 Advanced Disruptor Cannon

Slower than the Disruptor but much more powerful, the Disruptor Cannon is superb for attacking shields as well as subsystems, but it consumes a good deal of energy. Use sparingly.

Damage:	**25**
Rate of Fire:	**1.6**
Armor Damage Multiple:	**0**
Shield Damage Multiple:	**1**
Subsystem Damage Multiple:	**1**
Energy Consumed:	**0.75**

GTW-15 Avenger

The Avenger is a radar-based, rapid-firing cannon. It's best utilized when defending yourself against nearby Shivan or Vasudan spacecraft.

Damage:	**16**
Rate of Fire:	**4**
Armor Damage Multiple:	**1.25**
Shield Damage Multiple:	**0.85**
Subsystem Damage Multiple:	**0.35**
Energy Consumed:	**0.3**

GTW-32 FLAIL

The *Flail* is a rapid-firing krypton laser that is recommended as a tactical weapon for distracting enemy ships. Use sparingly as a weapon of destruction.

Damage:	2
Rate of Fire:	6.6
Armor Damage Multiple:	0.5
Shield Damage Multiple:	4
Subsystem Damage Multiple:	0.2
Energy Consumed:	0.1

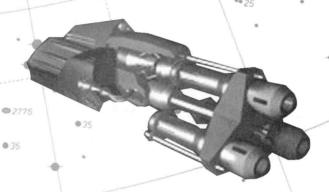

GTW-5 PROMETHEUS

The Prometheus is an argon laser gun named after the Titan who, challenging the gods, bestowed humankind with fire. Get to know your friend—he is one of the most effective of Terran primary weapons.

Damage:	20
Rate of Fire:	3.3
Armor Damage Multiple:	1.3
Shield Damage Multiple:	0.7
Subsystem Damage Multiple:	0.35
Energy Consumed:	0.4

GTW-7 BANSHEE

It ain't over till the old lady screams! The Banshee, according to Gaelic folk-lore, was an old lady whose scream, if heard, meant imminent death for those within audible range. This electromagnetic weapon was named after her because of its wailing sound, not to mention its devastating consequences.

Damage:	26
Rate of Fire:	2.5
Armor Damage Multiple:	0.7
Shield Damage Multiple:	1.2
Subsystem Damage Multiple:	.35
Energy Consumed:	0.8

GTW 99 RAILGUN

If you want to see power, take a look at this baby. The Railgun is one of the GTA's prime top secret weapons. Sorry guys, you can't take notes on this one: it's classified material.

Damage:	40
Rate of Fire:	3.3
Armor Damage Multiple:	1
Shield Damage Multiple:	1
Subsystem Damage Multiple:	1
Energy Consumed:	5

GTW-99 SHIELD BREAKER

Another classified cannon of destruction, the Shield Breaker is especially designed for those hard-to-get-rid-of shield systems.

Damage:	40
Rate of Fire:	3.3
Armor Damage Multiple:	0
Shield Damage Multiple:	1
Subsystem Damage Multiple:	0
Energy Consumed:	0.2

TERRAN LASER TURRET

The Terran Laser Turret is the basic turret laser found on most Terran capital ships. Don't get caught in its unfriendly, friendly fire

Damage:	35
Rate of Fire:	1
Armor Damage Multiple:	1.25
Shield Damage Multiple:	0.85
Subsystem Damage Multiple:	.75
Energy Consumed:	0.3

TERRAN LIGHT LASER TURRET

The Terran Light Laser Turret is a basic light turret laser found on some Terran ships. It is not, however, quite as potent against shields and subsystems as the regular laser turret.

Damage: 35
Rate of Fire: 1
Armor Damage Multiple: 1.25
Shield Damage Multiple: 0.15
Subsystem Damage Multiple: .15
Energy Consumed: 0.3

VASUDAN LIGHT LASER

The Vasudan Light Laser is quick and the deadly. A laser cannon of substantial caliber, this gun's notoriety lies in its infamous firing rate. It's quite a pistol but not in the same league as the Shivan lasers.

Damage: 5
Rate of Fire: 2
Armor Damage Multiple: 1
Shield Damage Multiple: 0.2
Subsystem Damage Multiple: 1
Energy Consumed: 0.3

SHIVAN LIGHT LASER

This Shivan laser has some kick but not near as much as its cousins. Still, don't take it too lightly (pun intended).

Damage:	8
Rate of Fire:	3.3
Armor Damage Multiple:	1
Shield Damage Multiple:	1
Subsystem Damage Multiple:	1
Energy Consumed:	0.3

SHIVAN HEAVY LASER

The Shivan Heavy Laser is fast and dangerous. This weapon makes even the Vasudan Light Laser look lame.

Damage:	15
Rate of Fire:	20
Armor Damage Multiple:	1
Shield Damage Multiple:	1
Subsystem Damage Multiple:	1
Energy Consumed:	0.4

SHIVAN MEGA LASER

This cannon can smoke your ship if you don't watch out. The drawback for Shivan pilots is the laser's large consumption of ship energy.

Damage:	**30**
Rate of Fire:	**1.5**
Armor Damage Multiple:	1
Shield Damage Multiple:	0.6
Subsystem Damage Multiple:	1
Energy Consumed:	0.9

SHIVAN TURRET LASER

Holy Dynamite, the enemy sure does know how to throw a punch! Duck from the Shivan Turret Laser if you don't want your hull to be vaporized.

Damage:	**60**
Rate of Fire:	**1.2**
Armor Damage Multiple:	1
Shield Damage Multiple:	1
Subsystem Damage Multiple:	1
Energy Consumed:	0.3

SHIVAN SUPER LASER

The Shivan Super Laser is the most powerful laser gun in the universe—hands down. The Shivans' "big daddy" can blow you to smithereens, EASILY!

Damage:	15,000
Rate of Fire:	10
Armor Damage Multiple:	1
Shield Damage Multiple:	1
Subsystem Damage Multiple:	1
Energy Consumed:	0.3

SECONDARY WEAPONS

This category includes all missile-based warheads and bombs.

GTM MX-50

The MX-50, a 16.5 kiloton missile, is better against hulls than shields. Using infrared tracking, the MX-50 rarely misses when fired in close at the target's rear aspect. Use it often.

Damage:	25
Rate of Fire:	1.5
Armor Damage Multiple:	1
Shield Damage Multiple:	0.4
Subsystem Damage Multiple:	1
Energy Consumed:	0

GTM-31 Disruptor Missile

Few ships can carry these, so learn how to use them. The D-Missile is designed to temporarily disable an enemy ship's subsystems.

Damage:	1
Rate of Fire:	5
Armor Damage Multiple:	0
Shield Damage Multiple:	0
Subsystem Damage Multiple:	1
Energy Consumed:	0

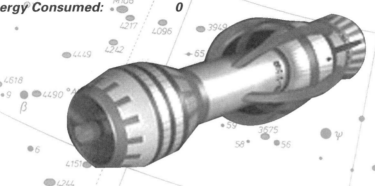

GTM-2 Fury

Furies are best to launch in a swarm at nearby spacecraft. They are dumb missiles, so wait until you're close before firing them. Use primarily for distraction.

Damage:	30
Rate of Fire:	3.3
Armor Damage Multiple:	1
Shield Damage Multiple:	0.5
Subsystem Damage Multiple:	0.6
Energy Consumed:	0

GTM-2 Hornet

The GTA engineered the Hornet's four missile bursts as an offensive equivalent of the Fury. With its infrared tracking, the Hornet's "sting" guarantees one or two hits per shot.

Damage:	65
Rate of Fire:	2
Armor Damage Multiple:	2
Shield Damage Multiple:	1
Subsystem Damage Multiple:	0.3
Energy Consumed:	0

GTM-9 Interceptor

The Interceptor is a fast, laser-tracking, medium payload missile best used against smaller ships. It's also a favorite for beginners because of its grace and ease. You can lock on to a target at 1,000 meters. Be advised, however; the longer the missile's flight, the greater chance the target has of avoiding it.

Damage:	175
Rate of Fire:	1
Armor Damage Multiple:	1
Shield Damage Multiple:	0.8
Subsystem Damage Multiple:	0.5
Energy Consumed:	0

GTM PHOENIX V

Perhaps the most dangerous missile in the Terran arsenal, the Phoenix V packs a lot of bang for your buck. Because of its heavy payload (50 kilotons), this warhead is not quite as fast as its little brother, the Interceptor.

Damage:	**350**
Rate of Fire:	**5**
Armor Damage Multiple:	**1**
Shield Damage Multiple:	**0.5**
Subsystem Damage Multiple:	**0.8**
Energy Consumed:	**0**

GTM-1 SYNAPTIC BOMB

The Synaptic Bomb is different from the others due to a special feature. The Synaptic Bomb is a missile propulsion unit that launches bomblets at its target. Within 100 meters or so, these bomblets direct themselves at their enemy from sphere formation.

Damage:	**60**
Rate of Fire:	**1 per 5 seconds**
Armor Damage Multiple:	**1**
Shield Damage Multiple:	**0.75**
Subsystem Damage Multiple:	**1**
Energy Consumed:	**0**

GTM-43 Stiletto

The Stiletto is an excellent (and perhaps the best) choice for taking out an enemy craft's subsystems. Its size, however, limits the number that can be carried.

Damage:	475
Rate of Fire:	1 per 2 seconds
Armor Damage Multiple:	0.01
Shield Damage Multiple:	0
Subsystem Damage Multiple:	1
Energy Consumed:	0

GTM-3 Tsunami

The Tsunami is an anti-matter bomb that is the weapon of choice for Terrans against larger targets. GTA pilots are limited to carrying six on board unless they have special authorization. Note that Shivans use similar anti-matter warfare in what the GTA dubs an "unknown bomb."

Damage:	1500
Rate of Fire:	1 per 20 seconds
Armor Damage Multiple:	1
Shield Damage Multiple:	0.02
Subsystem Damage Multiple:	2
Energy Consumed:	0

GTM-N1 Harbinger

The Harbinger, a 5000 megaton "Harbinger of destruction," is a fusion bomb souped-up with three outer fission bombs. Shivans use the same equivalent in another one of their so-called "unknown bombs." Warning: The shock wave resulting from one of these things is potentially fatal for anyone caught in its path.

Damage:	**3200**
Rate of Fire:	**1 per 30 seconds**
Armor Damage Multiple:	**1**
Shield Damage Multiple:	**0.01**
Subsystem Damage Multiple:	**1**
Energy Consumed:	**0**

Fusion Mortar

The Fusion Mortar is a powerful weapon carried by some capital ships.

Damage:	**80**
Rate of Fire:	**1**
Armor Damage Multiple:	**1**
Shield Damage Multiple:	**1**
Subsystem Damage Multiple:	**1**
Energy Consumed:	**0**

VASUDAN FLUX CANNON

A mild version of the GTA's Tsunami, the Vasudan Flux Cannon capital-
izes on the new anti-matter technology.

Damage:	500
Rate of Fire:	1 per 5 seconds
Armor Damage Multiple:	1
Shield Damage Multiple:	0.1
Subsystem Damage Multiple:	1
Energy Consumed:	0

SHIVAN CLUSTER

The Shivan Cluster is, in short, a better version of the Synaptic. The
cluster's fire power is four times that of its Terran counterpart.

Damage:	60
Rate of Fire:	20
Armor Damage Multiple:	1
Shield Damage Multiple:	0.75
Subsystem Damage Multiple:	1
Energy Consumed:	0

FIGHTERKILLER

The FighterKiller is a capital-ship-launched version of the Terran Interceptor. Despite its speed though, it lacks much of the Interceptor's bite.

Damage:	100
Rate of Fire:	5
Armor Damage Multiple:	1
Shield Damage Multiple:	.8
Subsystem Damage Multiple:	.5
Energy Consumed:	0

SWARMER

The Swarmer is another eapon found exclusively on capital ships. Similar in design to the Hornet, this offensive missile-based weapon fires a burst of warheads at the opposition. It surpasses the Hornet in rate of fire but lags behind in damage power.

Damage:	45
Rate of Fire:	15
Armor Damage Multiple:	2
Shield Damage Multiple:	1
Subsystem Damage Multiple:	0.3
Energy Consumed:	0

Well, you've learned about spacecraft, weapons, and miscellaneous stuff. Now, turn the page and learn to fly crooked and hard, shoot straight and fast, and wax some aliens.

THE ART
OF WAR

Chapter 6: The Art of War—General Piloting Strategies

As you all know, Descent: FreeSpace is not an exercise in problem solving, it is a game of skill. And because skill is the deciding factor, there are no trick solutions to the missions. To win most of the battles of Descent: FreeSpace, you need to know how to fly (and fight) a space fighter.

That's what this chapter is all about…fighting a space fighter. There are no real tricks, no hidden weapons; just a lot of practice and a good understanding of Descent: FreeSpace. We hope this chapter provides the understanding. The practice? Well, that's up to you.

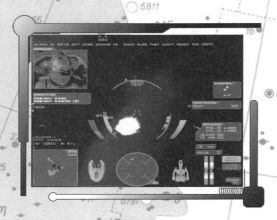

This is the goal.

Taming the Environment

We aren't talking about the harsh environs of space, but the taming of your gaming environment. Specifically, we are talking about winning the controller wars.

The Right Tool For The Job

Have you ever tried taking a bolt off your car with a pair of pliers? If you have, you probably didn't have much luck. Even if the bolt finally succumbed, I'm sure both the bolt and your pliers were a more than a little dinged up.

Piloting a GTF Apollo is a similar endeavor—it's difficult to fly that thing with a pair of pliers. Seriously, the point here is that to work (or play) properly, you need the right tool for the job.

In the case of Descent: FreeSpace, the right tool is a joystick—preferably a four-button, hatted joystick. Sure, you can fly your GTF Valkyrie by the keyboard, but you aren't going to knock down many enemy fighters that way.

Joysticks not only enable you to control your craft precisely but they also put most of that control in a single hand—a hand that is anchored in place, and that leaves your eyes free to search for bogies instead of shortcut keys.

Nevertheless, not all joysticks, or joystick configurations, are created equal. In the following sections, we'll look at some things I've found that help me to fly well.

Before we begin, you have to anchor your joystick to a stable surface. What's the use of putting all those controls in one place if you have to use both hands to steady it? The first rule to using a joystick effectively is to NAIL THAT PUPPY DOWN!

Of course you don't literally have to use nails; tape is preferable. Here are a couple of suggestions:

THE KEYBOARD TRAY METHOD

A lot of folks have keyboard trays that slide out from under their desktop. If you are one of them, try this: Place the joystick on the tray. Use duct, packing, or the U.S. Postal Service's Priority Mail tape to anchor the stick to the tray by looping the tape over the controller and completely around the tray.

THE NON-KEYBOARD TRAY METHOD

Not all of us, however, have slide out keyboard trays. Despair not, I have a solution.

Cut a piece of 1/4-inch plywood into a 18-inch by 8-inch rectangle. The dimensions are not critical; however, the larger the rectangle, the more stable your joystick will be. If your joystick base has a lip, drill a hole through the lip and screw the base onto the plywood rectangle. If it doesn't, loop tape around the joystick base and the plywood rectangle until the base is firmly attached to the rectangle. Place the plywood base on your desktop and you are good to go.

NOTE

Taping the edges of the plywood rectangle to your desktop increases the apparatus' stability. Remember, the goal here is a joystick that can be manipulated with only one hand.

Slaving the Joystick

Okay, now you have the stick anchored. You can dive, climb, and juke with the best of them. But to maximize the joystick you need to set its buttons to cover the most frequently used keys in Descent: FreeSpace.

I use a good—not great—joystick. It's a four-button, hatted *Top Gun*. After numerous missions, I settled on the following button assignments:

BUTTONS	ASSIGNMENTS
One:	Primary Weapon
Two:	Secondary Weapon
Three:	Target Enemy Targeting Self
Four:	Fire Countermeasures
Hat Forward:	Full Throttle
Hat Back:	1/3 Throttle
Hat Left:	Afterburners
Hat Right:	Match Target's Speed

The setup isn't perfect. I still have to target subsystems, enemy craft, and set zero throttle, on the keyboard. Nevertheless, with my joystick properly anchored, my other hand is free to punch up the various keyboard keys I need.

A Final Word

Relax.

You can't fly well with a tense joystick arm, nor can you see opponents through squinting eyes. These truths are often overlooked.

Rest your joystick arm on something other than air. If your arm is dangling three feet above the floor, only supported by your grip on the joystick, it will tense. When it tenses, your movements become jerky. When your movements are jerky, your aim is off.

Support your arm. Place your joystick so that your arm rests on your computer desktop. Barring that, rest your arm on the top of your thigh—whatever it takes to relax.

Are you squinting? Is that speck a Vasudan Anubis or a smudge on your monitor screen? If you answered "I dunno" to either question you need to do the following:

1. *Clean your monitor.*
2. *Turn down the ambient lighting.*

Descent: FreeSpace is a tough game. There's no need to handicap yourself by limiting your vision. So, tape down your joystick, clean up that monitor, relax that arm, and let's go dogfight.

FIGHTING

Descent: FreeSpace is all about fighting. To win, to move the campaign, to learn the story of the Shivans, you must fight, and fight well. The next few sections lay out the tactics I used in writing the book. Not all these tactics will work for all pilots, nor will they make you invincible. They will, however, make you a tad smarter. And that, coupled with about a hundred hours of practice, will make you a tough pilot to beat.

THE APPROACH

Dogfights (or strafing runs) nearly always begin with a head-on pass. How well you handle this nose-to-nose encounter may determine the victor of the fight.

THE CORKSCREW

The problem with head-on attacks is that you take a lot of damage on the way in. After all, it's easy for the enemy to aim at an incoming target that's flying straight and level. On the other hand, it's hard to hit what your are attacking if you fly erratically. The corkscrew is a compromise.

To corkscrew, press the Insert key and tilt your joystick to one side. This rolls your ship around the fuselage without turning away from your intended destination (which is the target). Now, while holding the joystick's original tilt, move it forward and back. This will raise and lower your craft while keeping your nose pointed at your target (kind of).

If you were to now trace a line along your flight path, it would resemble a corkscrew. The semi-erratic path makes you difficult to target, yet allows you to bore in on your victim, and occasionally fire a laser-burst at your enemy.

THE SHIELDS

Whether you corkscrew or not, properly managing your shields can determine whether you execute a successful pass or just get executed. Transfer all your shield power to your front shields (by pressing the up-arrow key) before going head-to-head with your opponent. This extra bit of juice may be just what you need to protect your cyber-hide.

THE POWER

Speed counts. A fast fighter is a flying fighter. Before heading in to a head-on attack, shift power to your engines (again by pressing the Delete key). The more power your engines have, the faster you go and the quicker your afterburners recharge. The quicker you close with your adversary, the less time they have to shoot at you.

> **NOTE**
>
> *You can allocate more power to your shields by pressing the Delete key. The more power the shields have, the more quickly they regenerate after taking a hit.*

APPROACHING CAPITAL SHIPS

Not all capital ships are created equal, and even if they were, a few minutes in combat unequalizes the best of them. Keep that in mind as you attack Destroyers and Cruisers.

Approach the capital ships from blind spots. For example, if you have previously taken out the two aft laser turrets, approach the capital ship from the rear. On the other hand, if the ship has lost all its close-in defense systems, get in close, very close, and blast away.

NOTE

A last word on approaches: Use the sun, especially when flying against other humans. The glare makes it harder to spot your fighter as you zoom in for the kill.

THE FIGHT

The approach is over, now it's time to fight. This where the rubber meets the road, or more appropriately where the lasers meet the metal.

MANEUVERING

The goal in dog-fighting—from World War I biplanes to Descent's fighters—is to get on the other pilot's tail, and once you arrive, to stay there.

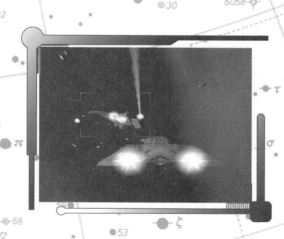

This is where you want to be.

93

Speed is Good

Speed is a pilot's best friend. Fast fighters can accelerate away from danger as well as rapidly close in on their enemy. To be effective, however, speed must be used wisely.

Don't get complacent. A predictable fighter is a dead fighter. Constantly vary your speed. Get on the afterburners when you are chasing an alien or closing for a head-on pass. Conversely, throttle back when you need to turn tightly.

But Not Always

The fighters of Descent: FreeSpace don't turn well at full throttle, or when the afterburners are engaged. They do turn well at 2/3 throttle. This is the speed you should punch up when trying to twist and turn in concert with your chosen victim.

Breaking Free

The computer loves to gang up on us poor carbon-based life forms. Sometimes, you'll be eating an opposing fighter alive, then out of nowhere, you'll start taking shots up the rear. And, no matter what you do, you can't shake off the bad guys—one of the two (your original prey or the newcomer) is always on your tail.

It's nearly impossible to outmaneuver two enemies in close quarters, so don't do it. Whenever two AI opponents gang up on you, engage your afterburners and blast away. Monitor your targeted enemy to ensure he is actually falling back. Once you've opened up a couple of hundred meters, turn and make a head-on pass. Frequently, one of the two will have flown off to search for new targets and you'll once again be in a one-on-one duel. If not, repeat the maneuver. If still not, try to get the heck out of Dodge.

> **NOTE**
>
> There is nothing magical per se about 2/3 throttle. The fact is that the slower a fighter's speed, the smaller its turning radius—at least to a point. Once the ship falls to 1/3 throttle, it begins to flounder a bit.
>
> So, if you're at full throttle and a Shivan Scorpion blasts by, punch the Backspace key (for zero throttle) and crank your fighter into a hard turn. The reduced throttle will enhance your turning capability, and you'll finish the turn before your speed drops too much.

Avoiding Missiles

Missiles are a pain in the rear...literally. Fortunately, your heads-up display will notify you when an opponent locks on and subsequently launches on your craft.

Launch your countermeasures as soon as you see the Launch light on your Heads Up Display. Next, turn 90 degrees off your original course and then light the afterburners. This will spoof most of the enemy's missiles.

Gunning

To live, you have to know how to maneuver, but to kill, you have to know how to (and what to) shoot. When are lasers better than missiles? When are guns better than lasers? When is a stiff drink and the latest copy of Rolling Stone better than any of the above?

Primary Weapons: The Killing Field

Primary Weapons are a lot of fun. I think it's the old "I-can fly-better-than-you-and-shoot-you-in-the-butt-while-I'm-doing-it" syndrome that makes them attractive. There is nothing complex here. You must get on an adversary's tail, stick to it like glue, and shoot them down. There are, however, some tricks to shooting down enemies and avoiding being shot down by enemies' primary weapons.

Use the right weapon for the job. For example, a GTW-32 Flail doesn't quite have the punch to take out a ship, at least not without landing a ton of shots. Conversely, it is extremely injurious (about 10 times more effective than an Avenger) to enemy shields.

So if you are piloting an Apollo equipped with both an Avenger and Flail, it's smart to take down your opponent's shields with the Flail, and then shift to the Avenger to vaporize his craft. Of course, you could simultaneously fire both weapons. That, however, would severely drain the ship's reactor power.

By the same token, use Disruptors to disrupt. Any weapon can knock out a targeted subsystem, but none do it as well as the Disruptor. Use the powerful stuff like lasers to knock down your opponent's shield, and then pump disruptor shells into the subsystem you want to disrupt.

Targeting a subsystem.

Regardless of whether you want to destroy an entire ship or merely disrupt a subsystem, make sure you are aiming in the proper place. You should place your HUD's crosshairs on the lead indicator, *not* the targeted ship. The lead circle calculates where the ship will be when your projectiles or energy bursts reach it.

Not only must you aim in the proper place, but in the proper manner. For example, if your opponent is at a 90-degree attitude to your ship (in other words, he is on his side and you are level), roll until you match attitude. This ensures that all of the bursts from you wing guns strike him or her squarely, instead of passing on either side of his fuselage.

NOTE

Note that the lead indicator keys to the most powerful weapon you are using. Hence, if you are simultaneously firing two types of primary weapons, it is not a totally accurate indicator of where the lesser weapon will strike. Nevertheless, with the nearly equal projectile/laser beam velocities of Descent: FreeSpace it's a pretty darn good guestimate.

Also note that you must not only target a capital ship subsystem you want to destroy, but also have a clear line of sight to the subsystem. It does you no good to pump shells into the belly of a cruiser if you want to destroy a FighterKiller missile battery on the dorsal side of the ship.

SECONDARY WEAPONS: THE GOOD STUFF

Sure, it's great to hang on a Scorpion's tail, squeezing off laser bursts until it explodes in a ball of flames. It is, however, safer to pump a missile into aforementioned Scorpion from a 1,000 meters away.

Secondary (that is, missile) weapons are some of the coolest armament in Descent: FreeSpace. Following are a few hints on how to use them:

- Use heat seekers, such as the MX-50, in close range. Fire them toward the exhaust of your target. Fire them when alien craft break away (usually as a precursor to another head-on attack).

- Fire Interceptors at medium (500–600 meters) range. If you fire them at max range (1,000 meters), the target can often spoof them. If you fire them at close range (100–200 meters), rate of change in the angle of intersection is too great for the missile to handle (that is, it can't track and turn quickly enough).

- Use slower, longer lock missiles, such as the Phoenix, against enemy bombers and capital ships. These are the biggest missiles a fighter can carry, and are your best bet for knocking out a big boy.

- Unless you need to save some heavy payload ordnance for heavy work, use your missiles as soon as you can. Missiles give you an advantage. Usually, the beginning of a mission (or thereabout) is where you are most disadvantaged. Use your missiles when swarms of enemy fighters are trying to kill you. Once you have thinned the enemy's ranks with a few well-placed Interceptors, you can trash the rest with your primary weapons.

KILLING CAPITAL SHIPS

Capital ships usually are tough nuts to crack, especially if you have to crack them alone. Whenever possible, use your wingmates to help destroy or disable the enemy cruisers and destroyers.

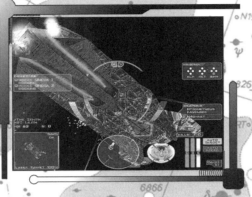

A Cruiser.

Never, if you can help it, bore straight in on a capital ship. Always use the corkscrew method discussed earlier, and make sure those shields are set to full front.

Take down one subsystem at a time. Start with the laser turrets or missile systems. Work on clearing one side, such as the bottom of the ship. Once the weapons systems have been cleared from an area of a ship, you can sit in that "blind spot" and engage the ship with impunity.

> **NOTE**
>
> Don't forget about the enemy fighters. It's best to thin the enemy fighter cover before you start on the capital ships. If you forget, an enemy fighter might just waste you while you're sitting in what you thought to be a "safe" blind spot.
>
> In some missions, you must disable or destroy a ship before it can warp out of the mission. In these instances, it's wise to target the ship's engines first. Once her engines are disabled, you can destroy her at your leisure.

Your Friends

Space is lonely—at least that's what they say. That's the bad news. The good news is that you don't have to be lonely alone. It's the rare Descent: FreeSpace mission that is flown solo.

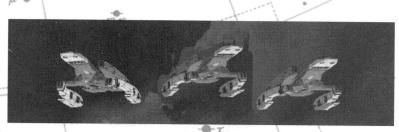

An Apollo Wing.

Using Your Wingmates

Interplay was nice enough to give us wingmates. It's only polite that we should use them. Use your wingmates to swamp the opposition. In target-rich missions, it's often best to target a bad guy and then order *everyone* to attack him. This brings down most enemies in short order. Target another, and move on. In this manner, you can quickly mow through a wing of aliens.

Don't forget your wingmates are there for you. If you're having a tough time with a couple of Shivan Basilisks, order them to cover you (press Shift+C). This will at least distract, if not eliminate, any extra Shivans on your tale.

Conversely, you may need to bring down a capital ship *and* fight a swarm of hostiles. I've found that the AI wingman works much better in dogfights than against the cruiser/destroyer crowd. Target an enemy fighter and then sic your wingmates on it. In the meantime, you can sneak off from the furball and get your licks in against the big boys.

THE END OF THE BEGINNING

You've learned the ships, weapons, and tactics—enough with the theory already! Now it's time to get to the meat of the matter. The ensuing chapters will cover, in laser blasting detail, how to win the missions of Descent: FreeSpace.

The Missions, Act I

CHAPTER 7
THE MISSIONS, ACT I

Okay, the waiting is over. Here is where the thrusters meet the vacuum. Follow along, and you'll learn how to bag some Vasudans and discover a spanking new sentient species in the process.

ACT I, MISSION 1:

EVE OF DESTRUCTION

MISSION BRIEFING

Pilot Attend: Welcome to the GTD Galatea. Your first assignment as a part of the Galatea's crew is to stand the third watch. You will patrol the area surrounding the GTC Orff. The GTC Orff suffered an engine breakdown in the Betelgeuse system and is awaiting repairs.

You will be on watch with one other ship: Alpha 2. Since this is your first watch, Alpha 2 will be piloted by Lieutenant Harrison, a seasoned veteran and top notch pilot.

You will begin your watch by jumping to Betelgeuse near the GTC Orff. We have detected a few Vasudan fighters in this system. Stay sharp. It could get hairy out there.

At the end of your watch, you will be relieved by Delta wing. Upon Delta's arrival, you are to return to base. Your primary objective will be to protect the Orff until the end of your watch. We expect you to carry out your orders to the letter.

You may confirm your ship hardware and weapons loadout for this mission in the weapons loadout. If found satisfactory, commit to the mission. GTD Galatea Quarterdeck signing off.

PRIMARY OBJECTIVE

✦ Protect the GTC Orff.

ENEMY FORCES

Virgo Attack Wing:	2 PVF Anubis
Cancer Attack Wing:	2 PVF Anubis
Aries Attack Wing:	2 PVF Anubis
Pisces Attack Wing:	3 PVF Anubis

FRIENDLY FORCES

Alpha 2:	GTF Apollo
Orff:	GTC Fenris

WINNING

This is a great mission to get your flight chops in order. Harrison is a competent pilot and the Vasudans come in slow.

NOTE

Have the LT help you If the Vasudans are giving you fits. Simply target a bad guy, press Shift+A, and the good LT will assist you.

The Vasudan Virgo wing are the first fighters to crash your party. Punch your afterburners and head for them straight away. Press the "H" key to target one of the nasties and match speed when he is 200–300 meters away. Lase him when he's close and pump MX-50s at him when he shows you his exhaust.

After you vaporize the Virgo wing, two more Anubis (Cancer Wing) arrive. Take them down and the twin Anubii of Aries Wing arrives. Once the Aries boys are down, the Vasudans get real serious. The next wing— Pisces—has three fighters. This, however, is their last gasp. Destroy the three Anubii, and the mission will end.

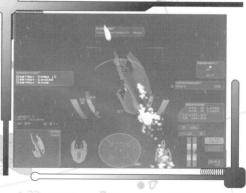

A Vasudan Anubis

Act I, Mission 2:
The Field of Battle

Mission Briefing

There have been a number of recent attacks by the Vasudans in the Betelgeuse System. They have been making strikes on Terran convoys en route to the Betelgeuse-Antares jump point. The Vasudan attacks have been staged from a nearby asteroid field.

Terran intelligence is certain that there are four small attack wings responsible for the attacks on your convoys. There have also been reports of a Vasudan ace piloting one of the Seth class fighters in the area.

You are to sweep the asteroid field and take out the four Vasudan attack wings. Be aware that the asteroids will be causing interference with your sensors. You won't be able to target the Vasudans until they are near, but they won't see you either.

If you encounter the Vasudan ace, you may use your discretion as to whether to engage him. Keep in mind that your primary objective is to take out the four attack wings.

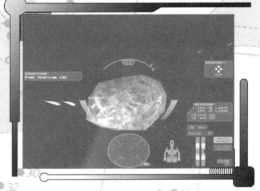

These puppies can be just as deadly as the Vasudan ace.

Primary Objective

✦ Destroy all Vasudan wings.

Secondary Objective

✦ Destroy the Vasudan ace.

ENEMY FORCES

Aries Attack Wing:	3 PVF Anubis
Cancer Attack Wing:	3 PVF Anubis
Pisces Attack Wing:	3 PVF Anubis
Virgo Attack Wing:	3 PVF Anubis
Vasudan Ace:	1 PVF Seth (Possible)

FRIENDLY FORCES

Alpha Attack Wing:	3 GTF Apollo

WINNING

Pop into the asteroid field and signal your Squad to form on your wing (press Shift+W). You'll notice several red flickers on your radar. Center one of them, and accelerate toward it. Keep closing until your wingman announces that he has a lock on Aries (or another) wing. Press the H key to target the closest Vasudan fighter, and you're ready to rumble.

Fire a salvo of MX-50 missiles while approaching your target. It rarely takes the pilot out (these are heat seekers after all), but usually weakens him. Fire him up with your laser once you get within 300 meters, and then target your next victim.

> **NOTE**
>
> Don't obsess with your current target. If you do, you'll hit an asteroid. Always keep an eye in front of your intended flight path. Dodge those asteroids; they pack quite a wallop, when they hit.

Once Aries wing is destroyed, follow the fuzzy red blips to Cancer, then Pisces, and finally Virgo Wing (the order may vary). Destroy them all. When the final Vasudan fighter blows, you'll receive orders to return to base. Ignore them. If you hang for a couple minutes, a new fuzzy red dot will appear. This is the Vasudan ace. Close until you can lock on, and then take him out. He's really not too tough.

ALTERNATIVE MISSIONS

This is easy. If Lieutenant Harrison died in the first mission, you won't be given the chance to confront the Vasudan ace. As a matter of fact, the ace won't be mentioned in the briefing. I guess the folks at Interplay believe that if you can't keep everyone alive in Mission 1, there is little chance in acing the ace in Mission 2.

Act I, Mission 3:
Small, Deadly Space

Mission Briefing

This mission will be a strike on a Vasudan Cargo depot. You are not to destroy the cargo, only the ships guarding the depot. When the area is clear, the remaining cargo will be picked up by your salvage crews for analysis.

The contents of the cargo containers is unknown. GTA intelligence suspects the possible existence of weapons, but it is more likely that the cargo contains routine medical and food supplies.

You will be flying this mission with Epsilon wing from the 3rd squadron. Delta wing will be available for reinforcements, if necessary. If you get in trouble, don't hesitate to call them in.

Reconnaissance missions have determined that there are typically two wings of Vasudan fighters guarding the depot. Obviously, the fighters are your primary concern. Recon also has determined that this is a heavy-use supply depot. Taking control of it will seriously impede any Vasudan attacks from this sector in the near future.

It is likely that there will be freighters in the area transporting cargo. All Vasudan vessels must be destroyed! None must escape, as they will surely bring reinforcements.

After you secure the area, the GTC Orff will enter and maintain watch over the outpost. Good luck, pilot. GTA command out.

Primary Objective

✦   Secure area until GTC Orff arrives.

Secondary Objectives

✦   Protect the Cargo containers.

✦   Eliminate all Vasudan freighters.

ENEMY FORCES

Freighters:	*2 PVFR Bast*
Aries Attack Wing:	*2 PVF Anubis*
Cancer Attack Wing:	*3 PVF Anubis*
Virgo Attack Wing:	*2 PVF Anubis*
Pisces Attack Wing:	*2 PVF Anubis*
Scorpio Attack Wing:	*6 PVF Anubis (2 Flights of 3 Craft)*

FRIENDLY FORCES

Alpha Wing: *3 GTF Apollo*

WINNING

As the mission opens, your wing man spots the Vasudan Anubis fighters guarding the depot. Hit your afterburners and close with the fighters. Choose a fighter, any fighter (leave the freighters for later), and fire off a salvo of MX missiles as you approach. Switch to lasers at about 200 meters to finish him off. Switch targets and repeat. Don't sweat the Vasudan reinforcements; just keep blasting. Be quick, however; if you fail to down the fighters in short order, the transports will check out. If you're fast, however, you might get three or four Vasudans before your wing-men splash them.

NOTE

If a Vasudan Freighter escapes, they will call in the Pisces wing. Although these are not major reinforcements, their arrival complicates the battle and signals your failure to achieve one of your secondary victory objectives.

If you are having trouble eliminating the freighters before they can jump, try this: After your wing vaporizes a couple of the initial Vasudan fighters, target freighter one and sic your wingmates on it while you handle the rest of the fighters. This normally will splash the freighter about the time you splash the final Anubis. Now target the second freighter and hit it with the rest of your wingmen.

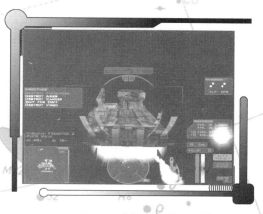

Vasudan Freighter

After the fighters are finished, take out the transports. Press Shift+A to target all wingmen on one transport. After it blows, get the next. Now enters the mysterious Omega. It docks with a cargo container and exits with weapons. There's not much you can do about it. If you shoot it, your fellow pilots will holler at you.

After the Omega departs, the final Vasudan wings arrive. Destroy them as you did the others. The Orff will enter, and the mission will end.

Alternative Missions

If you were unable to kill off the Vasudan wings in the last mission, the freighters will be armed, making the mission a tad more dangerous. Additionally, the Orff will enter damaged.

Act I, Mission 4:
Avenging Angels

Mission Briefing

Plans for the Avenger weapon prototype have been stolen by Lieutenant McCarthy. His transport has been located here in Antares. It has been designated Omega.

One of McCarthy's accomplices has been captured, and has revealed his intentions for the stolen plans. Not surprisingly, McCarthy intends to sell the Avenger to the Vasudans. His Vasudan contact has been named Rasputin.

Your squadron will arrive before the exchange takes place. You are to destroy all hostile fighters, including any renegade Terrans. However, we want McCarthy alive. Your ships have been equipped with Disruptors suitable for disabling the engines on the Omega.

Alpha wing and Beta wing, each consisting of four fighters, will be sent in to carry out the mission. You will jump in approximately six kilometers away from the exchange. Get to the Omega as soon as possible.

Expect to encounter significant resistance. Beta wing will focus on attacking the Vasudan forces. Alpha wing will be expected to disable the Omega. Request Beta wing's assistance if necessary.

After McCarthy's transport is disabled, the GTT Comet will jump into the area and dock with it. You are to ensure the safety of the comet, especially during the docking operation with Omega.

After the Comet and Omega have left the area, it is your responsibility to eliminate any remaining hostiles. Once the area is clear, you are to jump back to the Galatea.

Note that you will be required to engage Terran pilots. These pilots are traitors to the Alliance, and no quarter should be given. Thousands of lives are at stake. Do not hesitate to use deadly force on the traitors. They are your enemy.

If you encounter significant resistance or experience severe losses, Delta wing will be sent by Terran Command to assist. If further assistance is needed, call in Epsilon wing as well. Good luck, pilot.

PRIMARY OBJECTIVE

◆ Disable and capture the Omega.

SECONDARY OBJECTIVE

◆ Destroy all enemy fighters.

ENEMY FORCES

Aries Wing:	*3 PVF Horus*
Traitors:	*4 GTF Apollo*
Cancer Wing:	*3 PVF Anubis*
Virgo Wing:	*3 PVF Anubis*
Omega:	*GTT Elysium*
Rasputin:	*PVT Isis*

FRIENDLY FORCES

Alpha Wing:	*4 GTF Apollo*
Beta Wing:	*4 Apollo*
Comet:	*GTT Elysium*

WINNING

Target a traitor as the flight leader says his piece, and then order all fighters to attack it (press Shift+A, 3). There is a near and far pair. You want to target the near pair. Destroy the closest pair of traitors first and then handle the second pair.

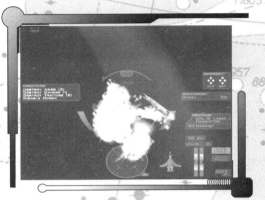

A traitor bites the dust.

> **NOTE**
>
> *Make sure you keep your wingman focused on the traitors, not the Vasudans. The Vasudan Aries wing will guard the Omega's rendezvous point until they are attacked or approached. You can limit casualties by swamping the traitors first.*

Now head for the Omega and wing Aries. Have your wingmen attack Aries while you disable the Omega. After it is disabled, the GTT Comet will arrive to take it in tow, and more Vasudans will jump into the fray. These are Anubis fighters of Virgo Wing. They will target the Comet, but you have them severely outnumbered. Take them out, wait for the Comet to jump out with the Omega, and the mission will end.

> **NOTE**
>
> *You can press Shift+P to order one of your wings to guard the Comet*

ALTERNATIVE MISSIONS

Mission 4 includes about 3 different scenarios. In the previous mission, if you were able to secure the system but let the freighters escape, you encountered those freighters again here. Suppose that Orff failed to show up in the last mission, even though you were able to secure the system. Well, when you arrive, you find to your dismay that Rasputin has gotten away. Finally, if in Mission 3 you secured the system but let the freighters escape and don't see Orff, then you will find that Rasputin and the freighters are long gone. Too bad for you.

ACT I, MISSION 5: OUT OF THE NIGHT, INTO THE FIRE

MISSION BRIEFING

With the Antares system nearly secure, Command has decided that the GTSC Plato will carry blueprints for the Avenger Attack Cannon through the Antares system. It will proceed to the Ribos System, where production of the Avenger will begin.

Intelligence has determined that only one Vasudan Cruiser remains in this system: the Taurus. If the Vasudans decide to attack the Plato on its way to Ribos, they will certainly use the Taurus.

The number of Vasudan attack craft in this system is minimal. Intelligence estimates at most two strike squads. If something should go wrong, the Plato is equipped with an escape pod. The escape pod will attempt to make subspace jump to Ribos.

Alpha Wing will provide cover for the Plato, and if necessary, the Plato's Escape Pod. The safety of the Blueprints is vital, and all Vasudan threats must be eliminated.

Pay special attention to any Vasudan Bombers that may arrive. Bombers will be the greatest threat to the Plato during this operation.

When you've cleared the area of hostile bombers, eliminate other threats and continue escorting the Plato to the Intersystem Subspace Node.

PRIMARY OBJECTIVE

✦ Escort the crew of the Plato to the node.

ENEMY FORCES

Aries Wing:	*3 PVF Anubis, 2 PVB Osiris*
Virgo Wing:	*4 PVF Anubis, 1 PVB Osiris*
Cancer Wing:	*3 PVF Anubis*
Shivan Reinforcements:	*4 Unknowns (SF Scorpions)*
Taurus:	*PVC Aten*

FRIENDLY FORCES

Alpha Wing:	**4 GTF Apollo**
Delta Wing:	**4 GTF Apollo**
Plato:	**GTSC Faustis**

WINNING

> **NOTE**
>
> *I take the Apollo on this mission. The Valkyrie is quicker, but won't stand up to the punishment the Vasudans dish out.*

Hang with the Plato until the Vasudan Aries Wing enters the fray. Ignore the briefing officer's comments and take out the Anubis fighters first. If you don't, you may be too weak to handle the rest of the mission. Once the Anubis fighters are junked, mop up the Osiris bombers.

Now the Vasudan cruiser Taurus decides to jump into your shorts. This would normally be a bad thing, but today is your lucky day. It, and most of the five craft of the escorting Vasudan Wing, will be annihilated by a wing of Shivan fighters. Terran command will order you to put an eyeball on the Shivans. Ignore the order, at least for now. Order your wingmates to guard the Plato and wait while the Shivans do your dirty work.

> **NOTE**
>
> *If the Osiris bombers slip past you, they may waste the Plato. Try ordering Alpha Wing to protect the Plato while you wade into the Vasudan fighters. Delta wing arrives shortly after the battle is joined, and you may have them assist in waxing the Vasudans.*

A sneak peak at the enemy to come, the Shivans.

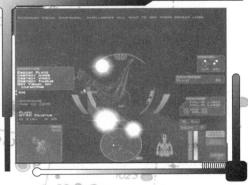

After the Taurus is blown and her escorts decimated, the Shivan will go home—at least it appears so. Unfortunately all good things must come to an end. The Shivans return. This time the Plato is their target. Neither you nor your wingmates will be able to hold them off.

After the Plato is destroyed, the crew will continue toward the node in the escape pod. Protect them as best you can. Concentrate on the Shivans. Attempt to sight a Shivan, but don't stress because of it. Often one of your wingmates will sight one for you.

After the Plato jumps, turn on the remaining Shivan with a vengeance (the others have usually warped out by now). If you haven't already, sight the craft and then shoot it down. Mop up the rest of the Vasudans, and then call it a day.

> **NOTE**
>
> Although your fire-control radar will not lock onto the Shivans, they will flicker on your HUD radar. Use these flickers to find them. Stay on their tail by alternating throttle. Remember that pressing the M key won't work unless you have a locked target. Accelerate toward them when they fly away, slow as they approach, and turn with them. Remember to lead them with your laser shots.

ALTERNATIVE MISSIONS

There is no alternative mission for this level.

ACT I, MISSION 6: PAVING THE WAY

MISSION BRIEFING

Due to increased encounters with Shivan forces, Terran Command has ordered the Galatea to the Beta Cygni system to monitor Shivan activity. The Galatea has taken quite a beating since her last repair, and there isn't time to follow the safest route.

The Antares-Beta Cygni jump node lies in the center of a dense asteroid field, making it one of the least used jump nodes in the galaxy. Standard procedure would have you circumvent this node completely, requiring two jumps. Now you have no choice.

Weapons systems have taken damage from enemy bombers. The Galatea should be able to make it through the asteroid field, but Alpha wing will be deployed to destroy approaching asteroids.

Alpha wing will fly point for the Galatea, and destroy any asteroids that cross its flight path. Asteroids that are considered a threat to the Galatea will be marked by white targeting brackets. Destroy these asteroids first.

After the Galatea has jumped out, you are to report to the GTD Bastion, stationed in Antares. The Bastion will take you to Ikeya for your next mission. Your wing will rendezvous with the Galatea in Beta Cygni upon completion of that mission.

In the event of an enemy attack, you are to cover the Galatea's escape from the system at any cost.

PRIMARY OBJECTIVE

✦ Escort the Galatea to the jump node.

SECONDARY OBJECTIVE

✦ Ensure the Galatea hull remains at 50% or greater.

ENEMY FORCES

Indra Wing: 2 SB Shaitan
Asteroids

FRIENDLY FORCES

Galtea: **GTD Orion**
Alpha Wing: 2 GTF Apollo

Not much strategy here. You just need to fly your butt off. Take position slightly above and in front of the Galatea. At first the asteroids come nice and slow, but don't worry, it heats up quickly.

Don't be afraid to use your afterburners. Bore in on each asteroid. Target the rocks closest to the Galatea. Ram them if you have to. Just keep an eye on your hull structure. Speed is the watchword for this scenario. Again, don't be shy about using the afterburners.

Busting rocks.

Target the Shivan bombers when they enter. Unopposed, they can wipe the Galatea slick in a heartbeat. If your are in their face, they will do less damage. And who knows? You may just bring one down.

The Shivans usually leave when the Galatea reaches the jump node. After the cruiser leaves the system, your job is finished.

ALTERNATIVE MISSIONS

If McCarthy was captured and Rasputin got away in the fourth mission, you will find that Galatea starts at 83 percent hull. That's a tough hit in this mission.

ACT I, MISSION 7:

PANDORA'S BOX

MISSION BRIEFING

Welcome to the GTD Bastion. The Bastion is currently on a special ops mission to investigate and acquire Shivan technology. This includes weaponry, shielding, and stealth technology. Intelligence has determined that at least one point of Shivan entry into our space lies in the Ikeya system.

At least five cargo depots of unknown origin have been located here in Ikeya. These cargo formations are different than any Vasudan and Terran formation, and are believed to belong to the Shivans.

Reconnaissance indicates that the depot is protected by six sentry guns on the outer edges. This depot provides a prime opportunity to gather more information about the Shivans. Their offensive activity in this system is at a minimum, and it is not believed that they will make a serious attempt to defend this depot.

Long range scanners indicate that some of these cargo containers contain unusual electronics. They appear to be similar to those used to give the Shivans their shielding technology. A short range scan of these containers is the primary objective in this operation.

Further reconnaissance indicates another container group might contain parts for a Shivan sensor array. A short range scan of this group should provide crucial data needed to adjust ship sensors to attain radar lock on Shivan fighters. Scanning those containers is your secondary objective.

You will jump in approximately six kilometers from the cargo depot. Proceed to the cargo depot quickly and eliminate all sentry guns. This will enable our freighters to collect the cargo after you have scanned it.

PRIMARY OBJECTIVES

✦ Use your sensors to scan the Shivan cargo containers.

✦ Destroy all sentry guns.

ENEMY FORCES

6 SSG Trident Sentry Guns
Numerous Cargo Containers
Arjuna Wing: 6 SF Manticore
Krishna Wing: 4 SF Manticore
Rama Wing: 4 SF Manticore

FRIENDLY FORCES

Alpha Wing: 4 GTF Apollos

WINNING

Of course, you knew it was a trap. But don't let that, or your wingmate's death, bother you. There is a job to do, and you are the pilot to do it. Order your wingmates to cover you, kick in the afterburners, and head for the cargo containers.

GTA command will announce the obvious (as if you didn't know it was a trap) and shortly thereafter, new orders will pop into the display. You must find the four containers that contain sensor arrays. Press the U key to target the next uninspected container and blast toward it. Remember, you must close to within 150 meters to inspect your target.

NOTE

Don't dally. The Shivans throw 14 fighters into this furball. It takes them a couple of minutes to reach you, and a couple more to waste your wingmates. After that they will hang on you like a cheap suit.

Ah, at last, the sensors.

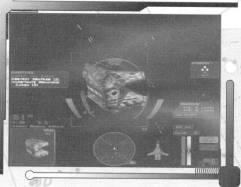

Target each in turn. Try to avoid collisions—you'll need all the hull integrity you can muster. If the Shivans come after you before your finished, fly defensively but continue to target containers. There is no way you can defeat the Shivans, so don't even try. When all four containers are targeted, break away from any pursuing Shivans and jump out.

NOTE

Tell your wingmates to cover you (press Shift+C) if the going gets hot. This may buy you the time you need.

ALTERNATIVE MISSIONS

There is no alternative mission here.

ACT I, MISSION 8: THE HAMMER AND THE ANVIL

MISSION BRIEFING

At roughly 1400 hours, you sent off a large convoy carrying what you hoped the enemy would believe is your only shield prototype. It was expected that the Shivans would attack the convoy.

The Shivans destroyed the convoy. What the Shivans do not know is that the convoy was a decoy. There were a total of four working prototypes, only one of which was destroyed.

You are to take two wings of fighters to escort the three remaining shield prototypes. The Shivans should think you are just another shipment headed to Beta Cygni. This is not the direct route to Earth, which should divert the Shivans from your true intent.

You are to accompany the freighters until the Vasudans arrive to escort them on the second leg. Do not leave the freighters until they have jumped to the Beta Cygni system.

The Shivans have hit everything sent from this installation. Expect resistance. Many pilots lost their lives today so that the chances for success on this mission would be greater. You will succeed. Dismissed.

PRIMARY OBJECTIVE

✦ Escort Shield Prototypes

ENEMY FORCES

Arjuna Wing:	4 SF Basilisks
Krishna Wing:	8 SF Basilisks (2 Flights of 4 Craft)
Aries Wing:	2 PVF Seth, 2 PVF Anubis
Cancer Wing:	4 PVF Seth
Rama Wing:	6 SF Scorpion (2 Flights of 3 Craft)
Durga Wing:	4 SF Basilisk
Vishnu Wing:	2 SF Basilisk
Pi Wing:	3 PVF Anubis

FRIENDLY FORCES

3 Cargo Containers (Alpha, Beta, Gamma):	TSC 2 Class Cargo Containers
Alpha Wing:	3 ValKyrie
Beta Wing:	4 ValKyrie
Omicron Wing:	1 PVF Seth
Mu Wing:	2 PVF Seth
RHO Wing:	1 PVF Anubis

WINNING

Okay, you know where this is heading before you start. Despite the briefing, you know the Shivans are going to be thick as thieves. Sure 'nuff, about one minute into the mission, the Arjuna wing appears. Not much to these guys. Target them and sic both wings on them. You can join in if you are looking for brownie points.

Ah, but here comes the moral dilemma: The Andromeda will hail your wing. She has been jumped by some Hammer of Light Vasudans and needs immediate assistance. Ignore her and focus on the greater good of mankind. You must get those shields to Earth. If you attack the incoming Hammer of Light folks, your cargo ships will suffer at the hands of a yet-to-be-announced Shivan Wing.

So blow off the Andromeda; it's too much strain. Focus on wasting each Shivan wing as it enters. About three minutes out from the jump node, six Vasudans will slide into your formation. These are not your relief, but the bad Hammer of Light folks. Vaporize them.

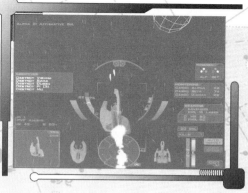

One more Vasudan for old time's sake.

A minute later, the friendly Vasudans of Rho and Omicron enter. For those without this strategy guide, they sound the alarm on the PI and MU wing impostors and another furball breaks out. Down the Hammer of Light pilots, and you've a free ride to the jump node.

ALTERNATIVE MISSIONS

There is only a slight difference in what happens here. The HOL ships may pretend to be friendly at first but fire upon you later, or the ships may just cut through this facade business and attack you (which is what they intended in the first place). Either way, they're coming after you.

ACT I, MISSION 9:

THE DARKNESS AND THE LIGHT

MISSION BRIEFING

The radical Vasudan splinter group known as the Hammer of Light has been conducting many surprise attacks on convoys throughout Beta Cygni. These attacks must be stopped. The Hammer of Light presence is to be eliminated from this system once and for all.

A Hammer of Light cargo depot, which is believed to be the primary supply center for all Hammer of Light activities in the system, has been located. This depot is guarded by a wing of Seth class fighters, as well as an Aten-class cruiser, the Ramses. The Hammer of Light does not have shielding technology, so this operation should be simple.

Your primary objective is to capture the Aten cruiser Ramses. You are to disable and disarm it with Disruptor cannons and then protect the Omega transports while they capture it.

Do not destroy the Ramses. The crew of the Ramses will be interrogated to learn more about the Hammer of Light.

After the Ramses has been disabled and disarmed, destroy all cargo in the area. The Hammer of Light cannot be permitted to resupply. The containers store Vasudan supplies useless to the GTA.

You are to lead Alpha Wing on this operation. Your ships are equipped with our new shielding system. In case of any unforeseen problems, await further orders from Command.

PRIMARY OBJECTIVE

✦ Disable the Ramses.

SECONDARY OBJECTIVE

✦ Destroy cargo depot.

ENEMY FORCES

Aries Wing: 3 PVF Seth
Virgo Wing: 4 PVF Seth
Rama Wing: 12 SF Scorpion (4 Flights of 3 Craft)
Ramses: PVC Aten
Taranus: SC Cain

FRIENDLY FORCES

Alpha Wing: 4 GTF Apollo

WINNING

Ah, but of course. You knew there had to be surprises. The Aries wing Seth fighters go down easy, but their replacements—the Vasudans of Virgo wing—have shields. Here's how to handle it all.

A Cargo box blows.

At the beginning of the mission, target a Seth from Aries and sic your wingmates on it. Continue down the line in like manner until the fighters of Aries and Virgo are down.

Ignore the Ramses and head for the cargo. Order your wingmates to cover you (press Shift + C) while you blow up the boxes. Meanwhile, back at the ranch the Shivan cruiser Taurus and the first flight of Rama Wing will be hitting the Ramses.

The Ramses usually is down by the time you finish the cargo and the Taurus warps out. Stick around to blast Scorpions, if you want, and then warp out when your hull gets low. At least you'll have fulfilled your secondary objectives.

> **NOTE**
>
> *I'm not sure if there is any way to disable the Ramses. You would have to wax the Taurus first. And that ship, with her compliment of 12 Scorpions flying cover, is darn near unwaxable.*

ALTERNATIVE MISSIONS

There is no alternative mission.

ACT I, MISSION 10: FIRST STRIKE

MISSION BRIEFING

The Cain-class cruiser Taranis has been chased from the Beta Cygni system back into the Ikeya system. It is low on supplies and, due to recent engagements, it is lightly guarded.

Long range sensors indicate that only two fighters and three bombers remain to protect the Taranis.

The Taranis is heading for the Beta Cygni subspace node, where it will probably resupply. This will allow for a small window of opportunity in which to conduct a strike.

Your primary objective is to disable and disarm the Taranis in order to enable its capture. This will be our first attempt to capture a major Shivan vessel. Three wings will be assigned to this task.

Alpha Wing will be flying Athena bombers. These bombers just arrived on the Galatea and are equipped with the new Stiletto bomb. The Stiletto is capable of destroying subsystems in one hit. Alpha's primary responsibility will be to disarm and disable the Taranis.

Beta Wing is assigned to escort Alpha and protect it from fighter attacks. Beta will fly Apollo-class fighters.

Gamma Wing will fly Valkyries and should engage any hostile fighters and bombers in the area. If needed elsewhere, they can be assigned to any task that you see fit.

After the Taranis has been disarmed and disabled, Omega transports will arrive and capture it. When the Taranis has been captured, you are to return to the Galatea for debriefing.

Do not allow the Taranis to escape or be destroyed. Good luck.

PRIMARY OBJECTIVE

✦ Capture the Taranis.

SECONDARY OBJECTIVES

✦ Disable the Taranis.

✦ Disarm the Taranis.

ENEMY FORCES

Arjuna Wing:	*2 SF Scorpion*
Indra Wing:	*3 SB Shaitan*
Krishna Wing:	*12 SF Scorpion (3 Flights of 4 Craft)*
Rama Wing:	*20 SF Basilisk (5 Flights of 4 Craft)*
Vishnu Wing:	*8 SF Scorpion (4 Flights of 2 Craft)*
Taranis:	*SC Cain*

FRIENDLY FORCES

Alpha Wing:	*4 GTB Athena*
Beta Wing:	*4 GTF Apollo*
Gamma Wing:	*4 GTF Valkyrie*
Omega (1 & 2):	*GTT Elysium*

Winning

As the mission starts, press Shift+C and direct Beta wing to cover you. Next, target the Taranis and tell Alpha wing to attack the Taranis (press Shift+A). Gamma wing will automatically seek enemy fighters to engage.

After the Taranis is disabled (the engines have been taken out), tell your wingmates to ignore it and attack the remaining hostile fighters. You'll have to plow through a total of 12 Scorpions.

Return to the Taranis and disarm it by knocking out all its weapon systems with your Disruptor.

> **Note**
>
> *You can target individual systems by pressing S; however, you must still have a clear shot at the system to disable it. In other words, you cannot disable the starboard missile launcher from the port side of the ship.*

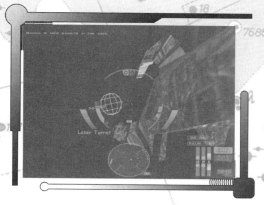

Targeting a Laser turret.

Now Omega 1 and 2 warp in and attempt to dock with the freighter. Unfortunately, about a minute later, Rama wing, replete with brand new Basilisk fighters, warp in. And, to lend the aliens a hand, Vishnu wing (Scorpions) bounds in also. Unfortunately, once you destroy these six fighters, six more will warp in. And then six more, and so on. Basically, this is the biggest furball of the game so far. The goal is simple—waste Shivans and keep them off the salvage team's back.

ALTERNATIVE MISSIONS

A similar mission exists for you if in mission 9 the cargo isn't destroyed and the Shivans arrive. The difference will be in the briefing before battle. The Taranis has survived the initial attacks, and it is flying to Beta Cygni to attack Terran forces. Your job is to stop and capture it.

THE END OF THE BEGINNING

The curtain falls on Act I. Stay tuned as the true depth of the Shivan menace is revealed in the next chapter.

The Missions, Act II

Chapter 8
The Missions, Act II

Well, it doesn't look too good for the GTA and their Vasudan buddies. The Shivans are stronger than the '96 Green Bay Packers and the Terran's John Elway has long since retired. Read on to look at some methods to stem the alien onslaught.

Act II, Mission 1: The Aftermath

Mission Briefing

The survivors of the Tombaugh attack must be evacuated from the Ribos system immediately. You do not have sufficient firepower to retake Ribos at this time. Your wing's objective is to escort the Iota transports.

Other wings will be accompanying this convoy. Alpha wing will be in charge of this operation and will have command authority. The convoy must reach the designated checkpoint. Escorts from this point onward will be provided by allied Vasudan forces, led by the PVD Pinnacle.

Hostile forces have been spotted all over this system and there is a good chance that our convoy will be attacked by Shivan fighters.

All hostile forces should be eliminated.

The PVD Pinnacle will be arriving at the designated checkpoint. This Typhon class destroyer has one of the most skilled crews in the PVD. It will escort the refugees for the remainder of their journey.

Help the Pinnacle until it has dismissed you, and then return to base. Many lives depend on this operation. Good luck.

Primary Objective

✦ Escort Iota to meet with the Pinnacle.

ENEMY FORCES

Arjuna Wing: *3 SF Basilisk*
Asura Wing: *4 SF Basilisk*
Bheema Wing: *4 SF Basilisk*
Indra Wing: *3 SB Shaitan*
Krishna Wing: *4 SF Basilisk*
Rama Wing: *4 SF Scorpion*
Vishnu Wing: *3 SF Manticore*

FRIENDLY FORCES

Alpha Wing: *3 GTF Apollo*
Beta Wing: *2 GTF Valkyrie*
Epsilon Wing: *2 PVF Anubis*
Iota Wing: *3 GTT Elysium*
Omega Wing: *2 PVT Isis*
Sigma Wing: *2 GTT Elysium, 1 PVT Isis*
GTFR Nelson
PVD Pinnacle

WINNING

This is another target-rich environment. The key to After-math is to quickly jump on the bad guys. If you dilly-dally, they will chip away at the transports and cargo ships, eventually destroying them.

Letting lose an Interceptor.

> **NOTE**
>
> *The Interceptor missiles will lock at 1,000 meters. At about 700 meters, fire off a couple at your intended victim as you run in on him. If a wingmate has already lowered your target's shield, a couple of Interceptors may just do the enemy in.*

Outfit Alpha wing with Apollos. They may not be the sexiest fighters in your inventory, but they pack a punch and can take as good as they give. Make sure to stock up on the Interceptor Missiles; they are sweet.

The first Shivans to test your merit are the three Manticore of the Vishnu wing. You can down these guys without breaking a sweat.

Next at the plate is the most intense attack of the mission. Three Shivan wings, including a wing of Shaitan bombers, attempt to swamp your convoy. Keep your cool, send the Vasudans and Valkyries after the Shivan fighters, and lead Alpha wing to the bombers. Once this threat is eliminated, you can breathe a little easier.

Form your remaining wingmates on your wing, return to the transports, and pick off the next three Shivan fighter wings as they enter. Sometime in the midst of your furball, the Pinnacle will arrive. Down a few more Shivans, the Pinnacle will release you, and the mission will end.

ALTERNATIVE MISSIONS

No alternative missions for the beginning of Act II.

ACT II, MISSION 2: THE BIG BANG

MISSION BRIEFING

Red Alert! The GTS Asimov and the GTC Ravage are under attack in the Antares system.

The GTS Asimov was working on project Tsunami, which involves hyper-reactive substances. These substances are extremely volatile. If the Asimov is destroyed, the reagents are likely to reach critical mass. Analysis predicts a shockwave of up to five kilometers in radius.

The station is in bad shape. You need to clear the area, and then transport the scientists out of there.

When the area is secure, the GTT Spomer will jump in and retrieve the scientists. After they have been safely evacuated, return to base.

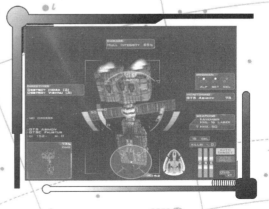

The Asimov.

You have five ships waiting in the hangar. You have no time to get them fully loaded out, so you'll need to use what you've got. Suit up! You're launching in two minutes.

PRIMARY OBJECTIVES

- ✦ Protect GTC Ravage
- ✦ Protect GTS Asimov

ENEMY FORCES

Rama Wing:	**3 SF Scorpion**
Indra Wing:	**4 SB Shaitan**
Vishnu Wing:	**3 SF Scorpion**
Krishna Wing:	**3 SF Scorpion**
Bheema Wing:	**3 SB Shaitan**

FRIENDLY FORCES

Alpha Wing: 3 GTF Apollo
Beta Wing: 2 GTF Valkryrie
GTS Asimov
GTC Ravage
GTT Spomer

WINNING

Rama and Indra wing pound the Asimov and the Spomer as the mission opens. Send Beta after the Scorpions while you and your buddies in Alpha down the Shaitan bombers.

About 30 seconds into the mission, the Shivans throw another wing of Scorpions at you. Try to ignore them. Remember, protecting the Ravage and Asimov is the task at hand. The Shaitan bombers are the greatest threat to their livelihood, so take them out first.

After you wax all the Shivans, the Spomer will warp in. It's quiet for a moment, then all hell, once again, breaks loose. A wing of Shivan bombers (Bheema) escorted by three Scorpions makes a run at your charge.

Again, assign Beta to the fighters while you and your Alpha wingmates take out the Shaitans. Once these Shivan are downed, the mission will end.

ALTERNATIVE MISSIONS

If you were able to keep only one Iota in flight in Mission 1, you will be presented with a different scenario. The difference: the Ravage is absent from both the briefing and the mission.

Act II, Mission 3:
La Ruota della Fortuna

Mission Briefing

Here in the Antares system you have detected a small HOL base of operations. Your squadron is being sent to eliminate it.

You will destroy all Hammer of Light ships, and then jump back to the Galatea. The Galatea will be monitoring you in case the situation gets out of control. Good luck.

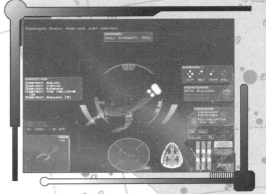

A Shivan Cruiser.

Primary Objective

◆ Eliminate all Hammer of Light presence in Beta Aquilae.

Enemy Forces

Arjuna:	9 SF Scorpion (3 Flights of 3 Craft)
Asura Wing:	4 SF Scorpions
Durga Wing:	4 SF Scorpions
Hellions Wing:	2 SC Lilith
Indra Wing:	2 SF Shaitans
Krishna Wing:	3 SF Scorpions
Rama Wing:	4 SB Nephilm
Vishnu Wing:	2 SF Scorpions

Friendly Forces

Alpha Wing:	4 GTF Apollo
Beta Wing:	2 GTF Valkyrie
Delta Wing:	2 GTB Medusa, 2 GTB Valkyrie
Gamma Wing:	2 GTB Medusa
GTD Galatea	

WINNING

This mission is a copy (or perhaps is vice versa) of the multiplayer mission of the same name. It's not particularly hard, but downing 27 fighters and two cruisers is not particularly easy either. Here's one way to handle that swarm of bad guys.

Hop into an Athena. Sure, the Medusa is a bit better for taking out the cruisers at the end of the game. You, however, are a bit better at taking out the swarms of fighters than your AI wingmates. If you have several real pilots with you (that is, you are in multiplayer mode), you can task them with escort duties and saddle up a Medusa yourself.

The mission opens without a sign of the Hammer of Light Vasudans. There are, however, plenty of Shivans to go around. Try to keep Gamma wing out of the battle. Their Medusas won't stand a chance against the Shivan fighters.

Take Alpha and Beta wing and tear into the three waiting enemy wings. As soon as you vaporize the last Scorpion, a new Shivan wing, Vishnu, arrives. They are a weak-kneed replacement for the just splashed craft, and their two Scorpions should pose no real challenge.

Now the Galatea will jump in, fresh from her own battle, and send the Delta Dogs to help. This wing comprises two Medusas and two Valkyries. Things are starting to look up until the main Shivan force arrives. Consisting of two Lilith class cruisers, three Scorpion Fighter escorts, and a wing of Nephilim bombers, these aliens mean business.

> **NOTE**
>
> Right about now the Arjunis wing warps in. Don't eliminate them. Their demise is the trigger for another Arjunis wing to enter, and so on, until nine Scorpions have been added to the fray. If you immobilize the last Arjunis fighter of this first wing, the rest will enter on a time delay vice the final destroyed Scorpion trigger. Make no doubt, they will enter, but it takes a little longer this way.

Send a wing to keep the Scorpions occupied, and then eliminate the Nephilim bombers. If you ignore them, they can wax the Galatea. Once the bombers are out of the way, have one wing engage any remaining Shivan fighters and send everyone else at the two cruisers.

Now is the time to let loose all the remaining bombs and ship killers in your inventory. Target laser and missile subsystems with your smaller weapons. After you knock out a couple, hunt for "dead zones" (those are areas no longer covered by the cruiser's weapons systems). If you find one, park your craft and blast the cruiser. Knock out both cruisers, mop up the remaining Shivan small craft, and the mission is over.

ALTERNATIVE MISSIONS

Hopefully you were successful in evacuating the Asimov during the second mission. If you allowed the Ravage to be destroyed or if it was absent in the previous mission, however, your Galatea will start at 83 percent hull for this level. Sorry.

ACT II, MISSION 4: WHERE EAGLES DARE

MISSION BRIEFING

In this mission, you will be assaulting a secondary supply and rearming facility under Hammer of Light control. It is located in an asteroid belt in the Antares system.

Intelligence indicates the main defenses will be two sentry guns and one wing of Vasudan fighters.

Recently, the transfer of cargo in this area has increased dramatically. It appears to be coming from the Ribos system.

This jump node to the Ribos system is approximately ten kilometers away. It will be the only means of escape. All of the Gemini transports and freighters must be destroyed before they reach the subspace node.

A wing of GTA Freighters will come in to recover remaining cargo. Keep the area secure until they are finished. Good luck.

PRIMARY OBJECTIVE

✦ Clear the area of all hostile ships.

SECONDARY OBJECTIVE

✦ Destroy Gemini transports.

ENEMY FORCES

Aries Wing:	6 PVF Anubis
Cancer Wing:	3 PVF Seth
Gemini Wing:	2 PVFR Satis, 1 PVFR Satis, 1 PVFR Ma'at
Virgo Wing:	4 PVF Seth
	4 PVSG Ankh

FRIENDLY FORCES

Alpha Wing:	3 Apollo
Beta Wing:	3 Athena
Iota Wing:	1 Apollo
Kappa Wing:	3 GTFR Poseidon

WINNING

Grab an Apollo; slap on some Interceptors, a Flail gun, and an Avenger; and head into space. Target Virgo wing and get to work. Use your Alpha wingmates to assist. About 30 seconds into the mission, the Cancer wing will dump three more Seth Fighters into your lap. Finish with Virgo, and then engage Cancer.

> **NOTE**
>
> Frequently, the best way to take out enemy fighters is to direct all fighters to target the ship you are targeting (press Shift+A, 3). By doing so, you'll take down a fighter about every 30 seconds.
>
> It's best to send the Athenas after the Gemini transport wing. Alpha wing, with your leadership, should be able to handle the fighters. On the other hand, the Athena Bombers are much more suited to destroying the transports. Link the Apollo's Flail cannon with the Avenger. Together they are a deadly ship killer; the Flail slices shields, the Avenger dices armor.

A metallic salad served, courtesy of your rapid fire Chefs: Mr. Avenger and Ms. Flail.

Just when you start to get a handle on things, the six Anubis of Aries wing warp in. These are good pilots, but a little dumb. They will often obsess with the Poseidon freighters, ignoring their tails. Pick them off, mop up the rest of the Hammer of Light freighters, and your work will be done.

ALTERNATIVE MISSIONS

The alternate mission is very similar, except the Gemini is closer to jump node. You will square off with the closer Gemini if your Galatea was at 83 percent hull in Mission 3. Otherwise, your current escapade will have a "normal" set-up.

Act II, Mission 5:
Tenderizer

Mission Briefing

In order to protect Vasudan Prime, the GTD Galatea will be moving from Antares to Beta Aquilae.

Alpha and Beta wings will provide escort.

The sentry guns surrounding the jump node were severely damaged in a recent Hammer of Light attack. Alpha wing will inspect the sentry guns to determine if they are salvageable. Beta wing will provide cover.

This is what happens to inquiring minds.

The Galatea will jump into Antares, reset its coordinates, and then jump to Beta Aquilae. Lately, the Hammer of Light has been attacking all ships passing through jump node. It is your responsibility to destroy all enemy ships that you encounter.

After the Galatea jumps to Beta Aquilae, you will be contacted by the Detiula Installation in the Antares system. There you will receive your briefing and move on to your next mission. Intelligence has specifically requested you and your wing for these missions. Good luck, pilot.

Primary Objective

✦ Patrol the area near the Antares-Beta Aquilae node.

ENEMY FORCES

Aries Wing:	2 PVF Anubis
Cancer Wing:	6 PVF Anubis (3 Flights of 2 Craft)
Gemini Wing:	2 PVF Anubis
Leo Wing:	2 PVF Anubis
Mauler:	PVC Aten
Scorpio Wing:	8 PVB Osiris (2 Flights of 4 Craft)
Taurus Wing:	9 PVF Seth (3 Flights of 3 Craft)
Virgo Wing:	4 PVB Osiris (2 Flights of 2 Craft)
	6 GTSG Sentry Guns

FRIENDLY FORCES

Alpha Wing:	3 GTF Hercules
Beta Wing:	3 GTF Apollo

WINNING

Another trap. Won't these Vasudans ever learn? Don't inspect the Sentry Guns—at least not at first. Inspecting the Sentry Guns reveals their Vasudan reprogramming, and turns them against you. Blow the first five away from outside the 150 meter inspection range, take the last one down to five to 10 percent, and then inspect it. When its true colors are revealed, blow it away. Once the Sentry Guns are silenced, the motherboard will consider the area patrolled.

> **NOTE**
>
> If you destroy all six Sentry Guns without inspecting at least one, you will fail the mission.

As soon as the trap is sprung, two Anubis warp in. Waste them and you get four more Anubis for your efforts. The Galatae jumps in and so do six Hammer of Light Osiris bombers. This, however, is only the tip of the iceberg. Over the next few moments, no less than 27 fighters and bombers will warp into the battle. Your job is simple: destroy them before they can destroy the Galatea.

> **NOTE**
>
> Save some Phoenix missiles. The Vasudan ship Mauler will jump into the battle at its climax and head straight for the Galatea. You must have the firepower left to take it down.

There is no difference in the missions for this level.

ACT II, MISSION 6: SHELL GAME

MISSION BRIEFING

You have reason to believe that the Shivan Destroyer Eva is in the Antares system near the Antares-Vega Jump Node.

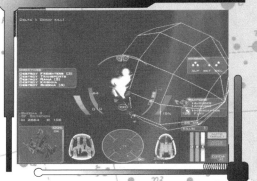

An exploding transport lights up the sky.

You will jump to this subspace node and investigate. Destroy all hostiles. Further orders will be given to you in-mission. Delta wing will be flying Medusa bombers and will assist you. If you need further assistance, you may call in Epsilon wing. Galactic Terran Intelligence out.

PRIMARY OBJECTIVE

✦ Destroy the Shivan transports.

SECONDARY OBJECTIVE

✦ Destroy the Shivan freighters.

ENEMY FORCES

Rama Wing:	*3 SF Scorpions*
Krishna Wing:	*3 SF Scorpions*
Arjuna Wing:	*3 SF Scorpion*
Bheema Wing:	*3 SF Scorpion*

FRIENDLY FORCES

Alpha Wing:	*3 GTF Hercules*
Beta Wing:	*3 GTF Apollo*
Delta Wing:	*3 GTB Athena*
GTT Dobbs:	*GTT Elysium*
GTT Harmon:	*GTT Elysium*
GTT Marcos:	*GTT Elysium*
GTT Stern:	*GTT Elysium*

WINNING

Hit your afterburners and head for the Shivan Freighters as the mission opens. Shift reactor power to your engines to tweak the last bit of speed out of your Hercules. Tell all your comrades to form on your wing.

The freighters will be in range just as Rama and Krishna wing warp in. Order your wingmates to cover (Shift+C) your attack on the freighters and wish for luck. If you get it (luck that is), you might destroy a couple of Freighters before the Shivans swamp you.

> **NOTE**
>
> *Leave Delta wing to continue attacking the cargo. Their Athena bombers can make short work of some of it while you wrestle the Shivans. Anyway, they wouldn't last long in a dogfight.*

Don't push it. Once the enemy fighters begin blasting you, engage them. You'll get back to the freighters later—like as soon as Rama and Krishna go down.

About a minute after you axe the last Rama/Krishna Scorpion Arjuna wing—with three more Scorps—warps in. Try to down a freighter before they do. Once Arjuna and Bheema wings arrive, however, jump on them like a trampoline. If you don't, they'll wipe the Shivan cargo slick.

> **NOTE**
>
> *You also can leave Beta wing at the Cargo containers and order them to protect them (press Shift+P). Beta will take a beating, but may hold off the Shivans until you can return from your transport-busting duties.*

After the Shivan fighters are downed, the Terran transports enter. All goes well until Shivan cargo container #3 explodes, taking the GTT Dobbs with it. The Stern refuses to dock. You are directed to scan the cargo. Do so. Your scan is inconclusive and the Stern docks, blowing herself up. As Natalie Imbruglia would say, "What's up with that?" The mission ends.

ALTERNATIVE MISSIONS

Again, there is no difference in the missions for this level.

ACT II, MISSION 7:
SCHEMES

MISSION BRIEFING

The Shivans have established quite a base of operations in the Deneb system. They have multiple supply depots scattered across the system, as well as several repair centers for their damaged fighters.

Each of these repair stations consists of a Cain-class cruiser and extra supplies. The Shakti is one such cruiser in the area.

All fighters in the area around the Shakti are damaged and in need of repair. This makes them easy targets. One of your objectives in this mission is to put this repair station out of commission. This will greatly reduce Shivan capability in the Deneb system.

One of the fighters being repaired by the Shakti is a Dragon-class fighter, designated Arjuna. The Dragon is the Shivans' most maneuverable craft, and the most dangerous.

Intelligence has requested that you capture the Dragon for research purposes. Since the Arjuna 1 Dragon is very low on power, it is in a weakened state, and is the best candidate for this operation. You must disable Arjuna 1 by destroying its engine subsystem.

After Arjuna 1 is disabled, the Charon will dock with it and jump back to the Galatea. You must capture Arjuna 1. You cannot allow it to be destroyed. To this end, you've equipped your craft with an advanced disruptor cannon. Use it to take out its engines.

Because this station is so poorly defended, you are sending only Alpha and Beta to attack. Alpha will cover Beta until the Shakti has been destroyed. Then Alpha will attempt to disable Arjuna 1.

If Alpha fails to disable Arjuna 1, Delta wing will be available. As Delta is currently guarding the Bastion, you will only send them in if it is imperative. It will take Delta approximately 10 minutes to reach you; however, we believe you can do it without their help.

Because you are custom outfitting your ship, you will not be able to customize your loadout. You have your orders. Dismissed.

PRIMARY OBJECTIVES

✦ Destroy the Cain Cruiser Shakti.

✦ Disable and capture the Arjuna 1 fighter.

ENEMY FORCES

Arjuna Wing:	**1 SF Dragon**
Indra Wing:	**2 SB Shaitan**
Rama Wing:	**2 SF Basilisk**
Vishnu Wing:	**1 SF Scorpion**
6 SSG Trident	
SC Shakti	

FRIENDLY FORCES

Alpha Wing:	**3 GTF Ulysses**
Beta Wing:	**3 GTB Medusa**

WINNING

Take your Alpha wingmates and lay into the Shivan fighters and bombers. Sic Beta wing on the Dragon. Make sure you tell them to disable, not destroy, it. Help out Beta once the Shivan fighters and bombers are eliminated.

NOTE

Remember, you can target the Dragon, assign Beta wing to disable it, and move on to another target. Beta will continue to target the Dragon even though your target has changed.

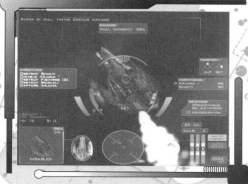

Enter the dragon.

After the Dragon is disabled, attack the Trident Sentry Guns, and then the Shakti herself. Remember to target the cruiser's weapons systems first (cycle through subsystems by pressing the S key). This reduces your Terran's pain as they take down the Shivan's capital ship. When the Shakti is destroyed (assuming the Dragon has been captured), the mission will end.

ALTERNATIVE MISSIONS

If you allowed some transports to escape in Mission 4, you will be given the task of an alternate mission for this level. For you, information about the Shakti and the order to destroy it will not be issued. In other words, it's going to be an easy day and a good chance to get back on track.

ACT II, MISSION 8: PLAYING JUDAS

MISSION BRIEFING

In this mission, you will be using the captured Shivan Dragon-class fighter on a scouting mission in the Deneb system.

The Shivans seem to be bringing in a large number of vessels into the Deneb system through the Vega jump node. This is in preparation for a preliminary assault on Vasuda Prime.

Because the Shivans have tight control over the Vega-Deneb jump node, you cannot send in a Terran scout. By flying, the Shivan Dragon will be able to slip in undetected.

There are four Shivan fighters in the area, maintaining tight patrol. If you come into close range with these fighters, they will certainly scan your ship, detect your presence, and open fire. Avoid contact with any of the Arjuna fighters.

Arjuna seems to be maintaining consistent patterns in their patrol. On arrival, observe their flight pattern and plan your course to avoid contact. In the event that you are engaged by Arjuna wing, return to the Galatea immediately.

Your primary objective is to conduct a close scan of all ships that pass through the Vega-Deneb Jump Node. This includes warships, freighters, and transports. Try to determine the contents of any cargo containers in the area, as well.

We have reason to believe that a Shivan Demon-class destroyer, the Eva, will be passing through this area. If it does, it is imperative that you scan it.

Remember that your fighter is only partially functional, and its flight systems will behave unpredictably. Be careful. Command out.

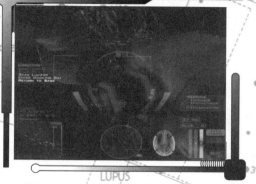

The Lucifer's docking bay.

PRIMARY OBJECTIVE

✦ Scan all destroyers and cruisers.

SECONDARY OBJECTIVE

✦ Scan all freighters and transports.

ENEMY FORCES

Arjuna Wing:	**3 SF Dragon**
Durga Wing:	**2 SFR Mephisto**
Kali Wing:	**3 ST Azrael**
Rama Wing:	**6 SF Manticore**
Ratri Wing:	**2 SFR Asmodeus**
Genma Wing:	**2 SC Lilith**
Eva:	**SD Shekar**
Lucifer	

FRIENDLY FORCES

1 SF Dragon

WINNING

Stay away from those triggers! This is one mission you can't win with brute force. Assign each Dragon in Arjuna Wing a hot key (Shift+F8, F9, F10, F11). To triumph, you must keep track of these fighters. Head for the Cargo containers and inspect the first two. When Kali and Duga arrive, split from your cargo duties and inspect the newcomers.

The Cruisers arrive next, followed shortly by Ratri Wing. Inspect the cruisers first, and then look at Ratri as they dock with the cargo containers.

The last two ships to make an appearance are Eva and the Lucifer. You'll have to stay on your toes to close with the Eva, but it's nothing compared to what GTA Command has in mind when you scan the Lucifer. *They want you to go into the fighter bay!* If you can do it, you'll put Chuck Yeager to shame.

All in all, this is one of the toughest missions so far. Remember to continually flick through the Arjuna wing and stay at least 1,000 meters away from the closest fighter, and also avoid the Sentry Guns. If you can, you'll be a hero. After all, it's the only chance you get to land on the Lucifer.

ALTERNATIVE MISSIONS

A slightly different version exists for those who did not destroy the Shakti in the previous mission. Four Dragons, instead of three, will go up against your forces.

ACT II, MISSION 9: EVANGELION

MISSION BRIEFING

The Eva has entered the Deneb system. She is fully armed and is poised to attack the Deneb-Vasuda Prime jump node. She is protected by Arjuna and Krishna wings. Alpha wing will lead an attack squadron to destroy the Eva. Alpha will fly bombers. Gamma and Beta will cover them.

We suggest that you damage the weapons subsystem on the Eva before you launch your Tsunami bombs. This will prevent the Eva from shooting them down.

You may need to call in a support ship to rearm yourself. It is estimated that at least 20 Tsunami bombs will be needed to take the Eva down.

Destroying the Eva is imperative. With the Lucifer in the system as well, you cannot tolerate the presence of another Shivan capital ship. Good luck.

PRIMARY OBJECTIVE

→ Destroy the Eva.

ENEMY FORCES

Arjuna Wing:	3 SF Dragon
Krishna Wing:	12 SF Manticore (4 Flights of 3 Craft)

FRIENDLY FORCES

Alpha Wing:	2 GTB Medusa
Beta Wing:	2 GTF Ulysses
Gama Wing:	2 GTF Hercules

WINNING

Blast in and swamp the two wings of Shivan fighters. We like to knock them both out before starting on the Eva.

NOTE

About thirty seconds after you destroy each wave of Manticores, the next will enter. This provides a wee bit of stress-free Eva bombing, but you need to hop on it quickly.

The Eva goes down.

Gamma wing will attack the Eva's main turrets by default. You should follow suit. Synaptic bombs are good against subsystems. They do, however, stand a chance of being shot down. Detail Beta to handle the other Krishna waves as they show. Launch your Tsunamis once the Eva's weapon turrets are knocked out. As soon as the fifth bomb hits, call in a support ship.

Let the Beta and Gamma folks fight the Shivan while you re-arm. Once you have a full load, renew the attack. Depending on how well your wingmates do, you may need to re-arm a couple of times. But finally, the big lady will go down and the mission will end.

ALTERNATIVE MISSIONS

Two versions for this level lie for those who failed on the previous mission. If you did not get to scan the freighters in Mission 8, you will be presented with poor intelligence in the briefing. No information regarding the weapons system or the types of enemy craft in that zone is known. If you failed to scan the warships but managed to stay until the end in Mission 8, you will be presented with the same dilemma as above *except* a cruiser's presence in the area will be acknowledged.

ACT II, MISSION 10: DOOMSDAY

MISSION BRIEFING

The Galatea is under fire from Shivan forces and looks sure to be lost. Long range sensors indicate at least four wings of bombers and interceptors. The Lucifer is also somewhere in the area. The Galatea must be protected until you can evacuate the personnel.

Good job destroying the Eva.

PRIMARY OBJECTIVES

✦ Protect the GTD Galatea.

ENEMY FORCES

Arjuna Wing:	*2 SF Manticore*
Indra Wing:	*2 SB Nephilim*
Krishna Wing:	*4 SF Dragon (2 Flights of 2 Craft)*
Bheema Wing:	*6 SB Nephilim (3 Flights of 2 craft)*
Rama Wing:	*9 SF Manticore (3 Flights of 3 craft)*
Asura Wing:	*4 SB Nephilim (4 Flights of 1 craft)*
	SD Lucifer

FRIENDLY FORCES

Alpha Wing:	*GTB Medusa*
Beta Wing:	*GTF Ulysses*
Gamma Wing:	*2 GTF Hercules*
Delta Wing:	*2 GTF Apollo*

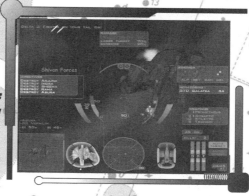

Man, that's a lot of Shivans!

WINNING

Face it, the Galatea is going down. There is no way that you can save her. The best you can do is deny the Shivan bomber's their glory, and force the Lucifer to bring her down. Oh yeah, and protect those escape pods. Here's one way.

Fight bombers, nothing but bombers. Send Gamma wing to down the scores of Manticores and Dragons. While you, along with Alpha and Beta, take on the Nephilims, pay special attention to the waves of Bheema and Asura wings as they carry the dreaded Tsunami bombs.

If you are lucky enough to down all the bombers, the Lucifer will waste the Galatea. (Don't try to fly into her fighter bay this mission.) Before the Galatea goes down, however, she launches her lifeboats. It's imperative that you escort them to safety. It is now, with the help of the newly arrived Delta wing, that you should target the Shivan fighters.

It doesn't take much to destroy a lifeboat, and the Manticores and Dragons have what it takes. Take out the Shivan fighters, escort the lifeboats to safety, and you'll have gained at least a moral victory.

ALTERNATIVE MISSIONS

No alternative missions exist here.

The Missions, Act III

CHAPTER 9
THE MISSIONS, ACT III

Things were looking plenty grim at the end of the last chapter. Most of the Vasudans had bitten the dust, and Earth is next on the agenda. Despair not, however; by the end of this chapter, one of two events occur: you will save the Earth or, you'll die. Either way, the uncertainty is over.

ACT III, MISSION 1:
EXODUS

MISSION BRIEFING

Pilot Attend: As you know, Vasuda Prime has been devastated. Your focus must now shift to the evacuation of the survivors. You are to take your wing to the subspace node cluster in the Alpha Centauri system.

There are three subspace nodes in this sector. They lead to Vasuda, Aldebaran, and Sirius. Civilians will be transported from Vasuda to Aldebaran.

Vasudan warships will travel to and from both the Sirius and Vasuda jump points. Because of the strategic importance of this system, you can expect the Shivans to try to secure it quickly. You will ensure the safe passage of all Allied vessels in the area. Additional orders will be sent to you as they arise.

PRIMARY OBJECTIVES

✦ Protect Allied Ships

✦ Secure Area Until Relief Arrives

ENEMY FORCES

Asura Wing:	*2 SB Nephilim, 1 SF Basilisk*
Arjuna Wing:	*4 SF Basilisk*
Indra Wing:	*4 SB Shaitan (2 Flights of 2 Craft)*
Kali Wing:	*4 SB Shaitan (2 Flights of 2 Craft)*
Rama Wing:	*2 SF Basilisk, 3 SB Nephilim*

FRIENDLY FORCES

Alpha Wing:	4 GTF Hercules
Epsilon Wing:	4 GTF Hercules
Phi Wing:	2 PVF Anubis, 2 PVF Seth, 3 PVF Horus
Theta Wing:	3 GTFR Poseidon
Zeta Wing:	4 GTF Hercules
Kappa Wing:	PVFR Satis
Mu Wing:	3 PVT Isis
Pi Wing:	1 PVF Horus
Rho Wing:	2 PVF Anubis
VC 3 16:	VC3 Cargo Pod
VAC 4 17:	VC4 Cargo Pod

WINNING

You get Hornet Swarm Missiles and Banshee lasers here. Equip your wings with Hercules, and load them out with Hornet Swarms and Banshee lasers.

Downing bombers is your prime goal in this mission. The Shivan bombers can take out the transports quicker than you can say, "Now wasn't that slick?" The first Shivan bombers to take a crack at the retreating Vasudans are the Shaitans of Indra and Kali wings. There are eight in all. Use the Hornets to weaken them as you head in for each kill. At this point in the mission, you can keep the Vasudans safe by aggressively attacking the Shivans.

> ### NOTE
> About the time that the first three Vasudan freighters (Kappa 4-6) exit, the Vasudans of Rho and PHI wings will begin trickling in. These folks will guard the Vasudans transiting between the jump nodes, but are otherwise worthless. You can, however, direct them to protect freighters or even to assist your attacks.

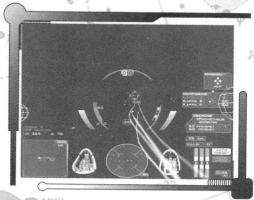

The sending end of a swarm of Hornets.

Once Mu Wing enters, direct PHI to protect them while you and your friends from Alpha/Epsilon concentrate on the newly arrived fighters and bombers from Arjuna wings. Destroy these aliens, and it's all downhill from here.

ALTERNATIVE MISSIONS

Unlike the other Acts, the beginning of Act III has an alternate mission. Things depend on the last mission of the second act. If you let the Lucifer shoot down the Galatea and some of the escapees in the pods were killed, you will not be able to arm up with Banshee lasers until the next mission— Sorry.

ACT III, MISSION 2:
LAST HOPE

MISSION BRIEFING

The PVD Hope is leaving the Antares system after an intense battle. It has sustained moderate damage and will be jumping to the Beta Aquilae system.

You are sending two wings to help cover the Hope while it is being repaired. The Vasudans are sending their own fighters to stand guard over the Hope, but it will be some time before they arrive.

The Hope should be in the system when you arrive. We do not believe the Shivans have enough forces in the system to mount a serious attack, but their strategies are difficult to predict. Good luck.

PRIMARY OBJECTIVE

✦   Protect the Hope.

ENEMY FORCES

Indra Wing:	6 SB Nephilim (2 Flights of 3 Craft)
Asura Wing:	4 SB Nephilim (2 Flights of 2 Craft)
Bheema Wing:	3 SB Shaitan
Krishna Wing:	2 SF Manticore
Arjuna Wing:	1 SF Dragon
Vishnu Wing:	2 SF Manticore
Durga Wing:	4 SF Dragon
Kali Wing:	4 SB Nephilim
Rama Wing:	4 SF Scorpions (2 Flights of 2 Craft)

FRIENDLY FORCES

Hope:	*PVD Typhon*
Alpha Wing:	*4 GTF Valkyrie*
Beta Wing:	*4 GTF Ulysses*
Pi Wing:	*2 PVF Horus*
Macross:	*PVC Aten*
Mu Wing:	*4 PVF Hoth*
Rho Wing:	*4 PVF Hoth*
Isis Repair:	*PVT Isis*

WINNING

Grab a Hercules and equip it with a Banshee, Prometheus, Hornets, and a rack of Phoenix missiles (more on the Phoenix later). Also, put the rest of Alpha in Hercs, but nix the Phoenix missiles (they aren't smart enough to use them correctly). I let Beta fly Ulysses. The Ulysses is significantly quicker, and they'll need that extra speed as they dash from one threat to the next.

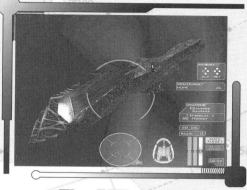

The PVD Hope.

Once the mission begins, head toward the Antares jump node with your wingmates in tow. The Hope will jump in and shortly thereafter, its pursuers arrive.

The second Indra wave and both waves of Asura will arrive in quick succession after you destroy the first two Shivan bombers. Designate the Vasudan wing, Pi, to guard the Hope, and split your remaining two Terran wings between the incoming bombers.

Once you've downed these bombers, Arjuna, Bheema and Krishna arrive. Put Beta on the Arjuna Dragon (he's a bad man with a laser cannon), and smash the bombers of Bheema with everyone else. After the Shaitans and Dragon are vaporized, mop up the Manticores.

> **NOTE**
>
> The closer you are to the Antares jump node when the Hope arrives, the sooner you can destroy the bombers of Indra wing. Your goal is to take out this wing of bombers before they can damage the Hope.

Now the Cain class Shivan cruiser arrives, as does the Isis repair ship. Order all fighters to attack the cruiser. This is when you can put those Phoenix to good use. Once the Lightning goes down, another Cain class, the Thunder arrives. At least the Vasudan cruiser Aten arrives to help you take this one down. Destroy it as you did the first.

NOTE

After the Lightning goes down, you'll have a short breather before the Thunder appears. It's a good idea to re-arm (press Shift+R).

Unfortunately, your trials are not over yet. Durga Wing, comprising four Dragons, and Vishnu, with two Manticore, enter, and by the time they're destroyed you'll probably be down a couple of fighters.

The Shivans aren't finished yet. In a last ditch effort, they throw the bombers and fighters of Kali and Rama wing. But alas, there will be much wailing and gnashing of teeth in Shiva-land. For as you finish pummeling these crafts, the Vasudan Mu and Rho wing arrive and the mission ends.

ALTERNATIVE MISSIONS

The alternate mission is almost the same here. The only difference is that the Macross isn't in the picture; that is, if he was killed in the previous mission. Common sense, huh?

ACT III, MISSION 3: A FAILURE TO COMMUNICATE

MISSION BRIEFING

Red Alert! The Beta Aquilae installation is under attack. The Lucifer has been sighted in the area. Protect it at all costs. Additional orders will be given to you on site.

PRIMARY OBJECTIVE

✦ Protect Aquilae installation.

ENEMY FORCES

Arjuna Wing:	4 SF Manticore (2 Flights of 2 Craft)
Asura Wing:	4 SB Shaitan
Bheema Wing:	6 SB Nephilim (2 flights of 3 Craft)
Deva Wing:	3 SF Dragon
Karna Wing:	4 SF Basilisk
Krishna Wing:	4 SF Basilisk
Rama Wing:	4 SF Scorpions
Lucifer	

FRIENDLY FORCES

Alpha Wing:	4 GTF Valkyrie
Cancer Wing:	4 PVF Thoth
Hope:	PVD Typhon
Aquilae Communications:	GTSC Faustus

WINNING

Kind of like a WWF match, this mission is rigged. When it opens, you see the Lucifer take down the Aquilae. Bam, right off the bat you have failed your primary objective. That's okay. Keep your chin up, there are plenty more objectives to meet.

For starters, you must escort the Aquilae installation escape pods. You can do this by killing Shivans quicker than they kill the pods. Take the newly arrived Cancer Wing, mate them with Alpha, and sic them on the Shivan Deva wing. Move quickly: you have about two minutes to knock them out before more trouble arrives.

The Beta Aquilae installation goes boom.

After these two wings bite the dust, Krishna arrives, followed shortly thereafter by Asura and Rama. Use Cancer on Krishna while you fly with Alpha against Asura and Rama.

Return to the Communications station and wait for Bheema and Arjuna to arrive. Fly out to meet them, defeat them (both waves) and the mission will end. At least you'll have saved the pods and the communications station.

ALTERNATIVE MISSIONS

A different mission lies ahead for those who let the Hope be destroyed in the second mission. This time, you will be presented with a new ship, the Pinnacle. But there is bad news: you have no Terran fighters to help you out.

Act III, Mission 4: Reaching the Zenith

Mission Briefing

As you already know, the Shivans have begun a massive offensive. They have completely cut us off from all of the outer colonies, and have our forces confined to the nine systems that form the heart of Terran space.

In what used to be Vasudan space at Altair, however, a group of Vasudan refugees has apparently unearthed records from a long dead civilization. Terran Command believes the information in these records to be of great importance.

You have located one potential weak point in the Shivan barrier encircling you. The Deneb jump node to the Ysusi system is being guarded by only one cruiser; the Zenith.

The Zenith is currently on patrol with just two wings of Shivan fighters, the Arjuna interceptors, and the Rama superiority fighters. We believe, however, they are able to call in reinforcements.

Your primary objective will be to destroy the Zenith. Take out the Zenith's communications system first to prevent it from calling in reinforcements. If you're unable to do that, go after all weapons systems, including turrets and missile launchers.

Alpha wing will provide cover for the bombers. Gamma wing will assist Alpha and will attempt to take out the communications system on the Zenith. Beta will be equipped with Tsunami bombs, and will be targeting suspected weak points on the Zenith's hull.

After you have completed these tasks, stand by for further orders. Good luck, Alpha 1.

Primary Objective

✦ Disarm the Cruiser Zenith.

Secondary Objective

✦ Destroy the Cruiser Zenith.

ENEMY FORCES

Rama Wing: 3 SF Dragon
Arjuna Wing: 9 SF Manticore (3 Flights of 3 Craft)
Vishnu Wing: 9 PVF Thoth (3 Flights of 3 Craft)
Zenith: SC Lilith
Krishna Wing: 9 SF Scorpion (3 Flights of 3 Craft)
Benedict: PVC Aten

FRIENDLY FORCES

Alpha Wing: 4 GTF Ulysses
Beta Wing: 4 GTB Medusa
Delta Wing: 4 GTF Hercules
Gama Wing: 4 GTF Hercules

WINNING

The only thing worse than trying to knock off a cruiser with a swarm of fighters on your back is trying to knock off two cruisers with a swarm of fighters on your back.

Trade in your Ulysses for a Medusa. Everyone else should use the default ships. Direct Alpha and Gama to engage Rama, while you and the pilots of Beta wing swoop in on the Zenith. Take down the cruiser's communications system first. This will cut back the Shivan reinforcements.

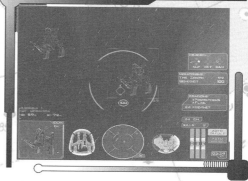

More Scorpions than the SOCAL desert.

> **NOTE**
>
> Don't be proud. As soon as you drop below 33 percent of your initial strength, call in the dogs of Delta wing. Use their Hercs to cover your attack on the Zenith (that is, target a Shivan fighter and order Delta to attack) or have them join your attack.

Once the Zenith's comms are destroyed, work on thinning out the fighters. By now, you will be facing parts of Arjuna, Vishnu (they came in with the Hammer of Light cruiser, the Benedict), and Krishnu wings. Destroy most of them and then target the Zenith, and order an all-out attack.

Don't stress on disarming the Zenith. It is disarmed if destroyed, so take it down and you'll have met your two objectives.

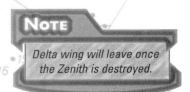

NOTE

Delta wing will leave once the Zenith is destroyed.

With the Zenith down, you can re-arm. Once you are finished, concentrate all your assets on the Benedict. If you take it out, great: if not, it will soon depart.

ALTERNATIVE MISSIONS

No different missions exist here.

ACT III, MISSION 5: RUNNING THE GAUNTLET

MISSION BRIEFING

As you already know, we are sending scientists to the Altair system to investigate records found on Altair 4. Command hopes they will aid us in our war with the Shivans.

The Rosetta is currently carrying the scientists. It will rendezvous with two transports, Omega 1 and Omega 2. All three ships should be arriving within a few minutes.

Omega wing will dock with the Rosetta as soon as they arrive. Oversee this personnel transfer. Then escort Omega 1 and Omega 2 to the Jump Node.

PRIMARY OBJECTIVES

✦   Get at least one Omega to the jump node.

SECONDARY OBJECTIVES

✦   Get both Omegas to the jump node

ENEMY FORCES

Arjuna Wing:	*80 SF Basilisk (20 Fights of 4 Craft)*
Indra Wing:	*20 SB Shaitan (5 Flights of 4 Craft)*
Rama Wing:	*16 Scorpions (8 Flights of 2 Craft)*
Vishnu Wing:	*10 Scorpions (5 Flights of 2 Craft)*
SD Lucifer	

FRIENDLY FORCES:

Alpha Wing:	4 GTF Ulysses
Beta Wing:	4 GTB Medusa
Gamma Wing:	4 GTF Hercules
Omega Wing:	2 GTT Elysium
GTSC Rosetta:	GTSC Faustus

WINNING

About 30 seconds after the mission boots, the GTSC Rosetta and Omega wing will arrive. Hot on their heals are the bombers of Indra wing. Order the bombers of Beta wing to protect the Rosetta, and wade into the Shivan bombers with Alpha and Gamma wings. If you are good, you can take them down before they damage either the Rosetta or the Omegas.

Unfortunately, That isn't the end of your worries—not by a long shot. In case you haven't already, check out the enemy order of battle. You will never, ever, clear the enemy fighters. Despair not; the mission is winnable, but you must fly in the face of adversity.

Once the Lucifer arrives, the fighters will start pouring in. Form Alpha on your wing and head for Omega, detail Gamma wing to assist Beta in protecting Omega also. As the fighters arrive, attack them with Alpha. Avoid straying too far from Omega wing. You must target the Shivans targeting Omega.

> **NOTE**
>
> Omega is Hotkeyed to F9 for this mission. Tapping F9 will target the two transports. Once the transports are targeted, pressing "G" will target the unit (or one of the units) targeting the transports. Once you have this information, order someone to destroy the offending Shivan.

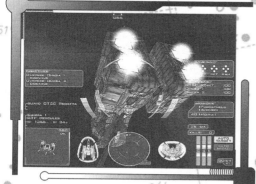

Continue to fight, downing Shivans as quickly as you can. Don't worry about the Lucifer. She won't normally interfere with the Omegas. If you're lucky, both transports will make it. If you are just good, at least one ought to get out.

The GTSC Rosetta before the Shivans get hold of her.

ALTERNATIVE MISSIONS

Two different versions of this level could find their way to you. First, if you could disable the Zenith in mission 4, a firing enemy freighter trying to aid its ally will meet you. Second, if you were unable to either disable or destroy the Zenith in mission 4, well, you guessed it—SHE'S BACK. Keep battling it out with the ship.

Act III, Mission 6:
Black Omega

Mission Briefing

You have successfully extracted the records from Altair 4. They have been partially deciphered, and are being moved back to Terran Space. Omega transports will once again be handling the movement of the scientists and the records.

Unfortunately, the Altair system is still controlled by the Hammer of Light. One of their flagships, the Anvil, is stationed here, and has gotten word of our presence in this system. It is currently blocking the vector to the subspace node.

The Anvil carries with it a powerful contingent of Vasudan fighters. Intelligence reports two squadrons: one of advanced Thoth space superiority fighters, and one of Horus Interceptors. These fighters have defended the Anvil well.

Intelligence also has detected the presence of a third wing of Vasudan bombers in the system. They will undoubtedly try to attack our fleeing transports.

Your strike force will once again consist of Alpha, Beta, and Gamma wings. Gamma will provide escort for Alpha while Alpha attacks the Anvil. Beta will ensure the safety of the transports and maintain our fighter superiority.

The Anvil must be destroyed. You are equipping Alpha with Harbinger bombs. These bombs require exact placement and careful maneuvering, but will do massive damage to the Anvil. Beta and Gamma must ensure that the Harbingers reach their target.

Your primary goal, however, is to ensure that Omega 1 and Omega 2 reach the jump node. Destroying the Anvil is the best way to ensure that this goal is accomplished. This mission is of grave importance. Do not fail, pilot. Good luck.

Primary Objective
+ Escort Omega to jump node.

Secondary Objectives
+ Destroy the Anvil.

ENEMY FORCES

Aries Wing: 9 PVF Thoth (3 Flights of 3 Craft)
Virgo Wing: 9 PVF Horus (3 Flights of 3 Craft)
Leo Wing: 2 PVB Osiris
Anvil: PVD Typhon

FRIENDLY FORCES

Alpha Wing: 4 GTB Ursa
Beta Wing: 4 GTF Ulysses
Gamma Wing: 4 GTF Hercules

NOTE

There are a lot of Vasudan Fighters in this battle (18 to be exact). You may find that attacking one of the Vasudan fighter wings (Virgo or Aries) not only takes the weight off Alpha, but aids in protecting the Omega twins.

WINNING

Not really a tough mission. Order the Beta Ulysses to down the Leo wing bombers, form Gamma on your wing, order Alpha to attack the Anvil, and head in with them.

NOTE

I like to immediately hit the destroyer with the Harbringers, and then unload my Interceptors and Synaptic Bombs. Don't waste primary weapon energy. Zip away and call for a reload.

Once Beta has zapped the bombers, instruct them protect Omega 2. Even if you lose Omega 1 before the Vasudan bombers are destroyed, you can still win the scenario as long as Omega 2 lives.

Continue pounding the Anvil until she crumples under the weight of your weaponry. Even if you fail to destroy her before Omega 2 passes by, the Anvil may be too busy with your attack to worry about her. When the Anvil is destroyed and whatever Omegas have departed, the mission will end.

NOTE

Be advised that bombs can be targeted and shot down. If you are having trouble destroying the Anvil with the headlong rush just described, try taking out some, if not all, of its weapons systems before you rain the bombs.

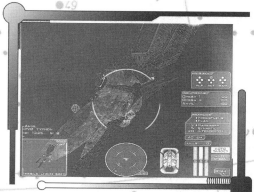

The Anvil in your sights.

ALTERNATIVE MISSIONS

If only one Omega made it through the last mission, there will be only one Omega in this mission. Makes sense, doesn't it? You will, however, need to be careful that you protect the lone Omega well. If you lose it, you lose.

Act III, Mission 7:
Clash of the Titans

Mission Briefing

You have few chances to stop the Lucifer. It is heading to the Sol system, but you have an opportunity to head them off at Sirius.

If you encounter the Lucifer in Sirius, hold it off until the rest of the fleet can catch up with you.

Primary Objective

✦   Escort the GTD Bastion to the Lucifer.

Secondary Objective

✦   Keep the GTD Bastion's Hull above 50%.

Enemy Forces

Asura Wing:	2 SB Shaitan
Arjuna Wing:	3 SF Basilisk
Bheema Wing:	2 SB Nephilim
Indra Wing:	2 SB Nephilim
Krishna Wing:	2 SF Manticore
Rama Wing:	2 SF Basilisk
Vishnu:	5 SF Basilisk
Tantalus:	SC Cain

Friendly Forces

GTD Bastion	
Alpha Wing:	3 GTF Ulysses
Beta Wing:	3 GTF Ulysses

Winning

Accelerate toward the jump node as the scenario starts. When the GTD Bastion enters, detail Alpha wing to protect her. Take Beta and blast toward the incoming Indra wing. The bombers are the main threat to the GTD Bastion; let Alpha guard her against the fighters.

When Indra is destroyed, Bheema will enter. Again, these

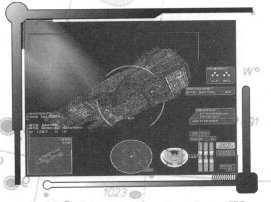

The Bastion fights for her life.

are a significant threat and need to be taken out immediately. After you have cleared (at least for now) the bombers, jump on the fighters. Alpha may have already taken a couple down, in addition to bombarding the Tantalus. Once these fighters are wasted, destroy the cruiser. There will be a brief lull in which you may rearm.

> **NOTE**
>
> *Once assigned to protect the Bastion, Alpha wing will attack anyone that attacks or threatens the destroyer. This includes the SC Tantalus. Frequently, they will destroy the vessel without any further prodding from yourself.*

Finally, the last of the bombers, Asura's Shaitans, will jump in. Destroy them and mop up their escorts, Vishnu, and the Bastion will jump into subspace. Follow her—you must jump at the Delta Serpentis node—and the mission will end.

> **NOTE**
>
> *You must jump exactly from the Delta Serpentis node; otherwise, you will not win the mission. I've found it's best to move to the node, stop, then jump.*

ACT III, MISSION 8: THE GREAT HUNT

MISSION BRIEFING

In a few minutes, you will be entering the Delta Serpentis sector. You will then commence the most important engagement in the history of our species. You will be responsible for the very survival of Earth.

Your plan is to rapidly close the distance with the Lucifer so that the Bastion can enter subspace close to the same time the Lucifer does. From there, you will enter subspace and attack the Lucifer.

Your task in this mission will be to provide cover for the Bastion so that it can quickly close the distance to the Lucifer. This is it, pilot. Good luck.

PRIMARY OBJECTIVE

✦ Make the jump to subspace.

ENEMY FORCES

SD Lucifer

Arjuna Wing:	**6 SF Basilisk**
Deva Wing:	**6 SF Basilisk**
Karna Wing:	**4 SF Basilisk**
Krishna Wing:	**3 SF Manticore**
Rama Wing:	**3 SF Manticore**

FRIENDLY FORCES

Alpha Wing:	**4 GTF Hercules**
Beta Wing:	**4 GTF Ulysses**
Delta Wing:	**4 GTB Ursa**
Epsilon:	**4 GTF Ulysses**

WINNING

Attention! This strategy is a spoiler!

In a sense, this is one of the easiest missions in the game. Alternatively, it's not. Without this guide, you'll spend the first few minutes of the mission vainly trying to clear Bastion's path to the Sol jump node. It seems, however, that no matter how many of the Basilisks from Karna, Deva, and Arjuna you down, the Bastion claims they can't make the jump node in time.

> **NOTE**
>
> *As mentioned earlier, take a Herc. Put your Alpha wingmates in one too, but don't stop there. The Ulysses is Beta's default craft. Change them to Hercs also. They will stand the constant lasing much better.*

Well, so be it. The Lucifer has departed and it's up to you to chase her into subspace. The Herc is the best craft for the job. It's quick enough to make the dash to the jump node, yet strong enough to withstand the early mission bashing.

Stay and fight until the Bastion tells you she can't make it. You are the best pilot out there, and every Shivan you down is one less Shivan sniffing your tail as you run for the jump node. Once GTA command tells you to go for the jump node, go for it. Tell everyone to cover you; Rama and Krishna wing will have reinforced the Shivans by now.

Put max energy into your engines for this run. It will recharge your thrusters quickly. If you use your thrusters wisely, you'll make the jump with time to spare, and the mission will end.

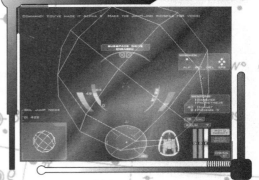

The Sol jump node: Victory is yours!

Act III, Mission 9:
Good Luck

Mission Briefing

Your objective is to take out the Lucifer. The Lucifer has five reactors located within its main hull. You will need to target these reactors for destruction. We estimate that it may take Harbringers to destroy a reactor on the Lucifer, so protect your Ursas.

You did well to make it here.

Primary Objective

✦ Destroy the Lucifer.

Enemy Forces

Arjuna Wing:	4 SF Arjuna
Deva Wing:	4 SF Dragon
SD Lucifer	

Friendly Forces

Alpha Wing:	4 GTF Hercs
Beta Wing:	4 GTF Ulysses
Delta Wing:	4 GTB Ursa
Epsilon Wing:	4 GTF Ulysses

Winning

Well, the good news is there are only two wings of Shivan fighters guarding the Lucifer. The bad news is that, with the Lucifer's firepower, she doesn't need much more.

NOTE

Be careful how you assign your wings. If you sic "All Fighters" on a target, Delta will also attack. It's best to target a fighter from Arjuna (such as Arjuna 2) and tell Alpha to destroy it. Target a new fighter and send Beta after it, and finally herd Epsilon toward a target.

When the mission begins, target the fighters of Deva and Arjuna Wing, and send Alpha, Beta, and Epsilon after them. Form Delta on your wing and sit back to watch.

It takes your wingmates about three to four minutes to wax the Shivan fighters. While they are busy, the Shivan fighters close—with Delta on your wing—to within 1500-2000 meters of the Lucifer. You should come straight in on her tail (the portion of the ship originally facing you on approach).

Once the fighters are down, assign Alpha, Beta, and Epsilon to destroy the weapon systems on the aft end of the Lucifer. Knock out at least the two missile launchers and main turrets. Now target the ship and tell "All Fighters" to attack. Yep, this includes the Ursas, but you have another plan for them.

Quickly cycle through reactors 2 through 5, and assign an Ursa to each. You take reactor 1 and destroy it with a combination of laser and missile fire. Watch your targeting cursor carefully. If you have a clear line of sight to your target, you'll get a cursor similar to that shown in the first screenshot. If the line of sight is blocked, your HUD will look like the second screenshot shown below.

Good to go.

Keep pounding the reactors. This, coupled with the general punishment the fighters are dishing out, will usually destroy the Lucifer. When the ship's hull reaches 2 percent, form all fighters on your wing and get out of Dodge.

When the Lucifer blows, she blows big, so you want to be a couple of clicks distant. Unfortunately, you'll have to detail one of your wings to administer the *coup de grace.*

Wasting your ammo.

These folks will die in the process. Once the Lucifer is destroyed, the mission will end.

TAPS

That's it for the Shivans. I'm sorry, too. I didn't like them, but I thought the campaign was great. I'm sorry to see it end. But, as Don Henley would say, "Put a monster smile on those rosy cheeks," 'cause we still have quite a few multiplayer missions to fly.

MULTIPLAYER MISSIONS

MULTIPLAYER MISSIONS

I loved *Descent: FreeSpace's* campaigns. The story line was absorbing and the introduction and subsequent integration of the Shivans was clever. Unfortunately, all good things must come to an end, and so it is with the *Descent: FreeSpace* story. Or is it?

Sure, the story is over, but the battles aren't. *Descent: FreeSpace's* multiplayer battles gives the game longer legs than a stork. I know I'll be attacking Shivan Cruisers with my friends for a long time to come. So, let's take a look at the missions and discover the best way to put those ugly Shivans, Vasudans and traitorous Terrans in their place.

MULTIPLAYER CAMPAIGNS

There are two multiplayer mini-campaigns. They can be played sequentially or their missions flown as stand alone scenarios.

JOURNEY TO ALTAIR

Important records have been unearthed on Altair 4 . However, getting there and back might be far more difficult than anyone ever imagined.

MISSION: REACHING THE ZENITH

PRIMARY OBJECTIVES

✦ Disable the Zenith

SECONDARY OBJECTIVES

✦ Destroy the Zenith

ENEMY FORCES

Aries Wing:	54 PVF Thoth (9 Flights of 6 Craft)
Arjuna Wing:	9 SF Manticore (3 Flights of 3 Craft)
Krishna Wing:	15 SF Scorpion (3 Flights of 5 Craft)
Rama Wing:	6 SF Dragon (2 Flights of 3 Craft)
Benedict:	PVC Aten
Zenith:	SC Lilith

FRIENDLY FORCES

Alpha Wing:	4 GTF Ulysses
Beta Wing:	4 GTB Medusa
Gama Wing:	4 GTF Hercules

WINNING

Another great single player conversion. Volition beefed up Aries and Krishna Wings, left the victory conditions the same, and came up with a great scenario.

Alpha and Gama should engage Rama, while Beta wing attacks the Zenith. Take down the cruiser's communications system first. This will cut back the Shivan reinforcements.

Once the Zenith's comms are destroyed, work on thinning out the fighters. By now, you will be facing parts of Arjuna, Aries(they came in with the Hammer of Light cruiser, the Benedict), and Krishnu wings. Destroy most of them, then target the Zenith and order an all out attack. Note that there are 54 Thoths available to the Benidict. Fortunately, their main job is to protect the Vasudan cruiser. If you don't bother them, they won't bother you. *Kinda...*

Don't stress on disarming the Zenith. It is disarmed if destroyed, so take it down, and you'll have met your two objectives.

With the Zenith down, you can rearm. Once you are finished, concentrate all your assets on the Benedict. If you take it out great, if not, it will soon depart.

NOTE

You can call for Delta to help in this mission also. Use their Hercs to cover your attack on the Zenith (i.e., target a Shivan fighter and order Delta to attack), or have them join your attack.

NOTE

Remember: the Zenith can target and destroy bombs with her weapons. So, if you have time, take out the weapon systems in one area before launching the Tsunamis.

NOTE

Delta wing will leave once the Zenith is destroyed.

MISSION: RUNNING THE GAUNTLET

PRIMARY OBJECTIVES

✦ Get at least one Omega to the jump node.

SECONDARY OBJECTIVES

✦ Get both Omegas to the jump node

ENEMY FORCES

Arjuna Wing:	**80 SF Manticore (20 Fights of 4 Craft)**
Indra Wing:	**20 SB Shaitan (5 Flights of 4 Craft)**
Rama Wing:	**16 Scorpions (8 Flights of 2 Craft)**
Vishnu Wing:	**20 Scorpions (5 Flights of 2 Craft)**
SD Lucifer	

FRIENDLY FORCES

Alpha Wing:	**4 GTF Ulysses**
Beta Wing:	**4 GTB Medusa**
Gamma Wing:	**4 GTF Hercules**
Omega Wing:	**2 GTT Elysium**
GTSC Rosetta:	**GTSC Faustus**

WINNING

Again, an excellent single player conversion. Adding ten Scorpions to Vishnu and changing Arjuna to Manticores were the only changes here. Soon after the mission boots, the GTSC Rosetta and Omega wing will arrive. Closely following are the bombers of Indra wing. Order Beta wing to protect the Rosetta and wade into the Shivan bombers with Alpha and Gamma wings. If you and your copilots are good, you can take them down before they damage either the Rosetta or the Omegas.

Unfortunately, there more Shivans inbound (just check out the order of battle). Despair not, the mission is winnable, but you must fly in the face of adversity.

Once the Lucifer arrives, the fighters will start pouring in. Form Alpha on your wing and head for Omega. Detail Gamma wing to assist Beta in protecting Omega also. As the fighters arrive, attack them with Alpha. Avoid straying too far from Omega wing. You must target the Shivans targeting Omega.

As in the single player mission, destroy Shivans as quickly as your lasers will allow—there are scads of them. At least the Lucifer normally won't interfere with the Omegans. Escort the transports to the jump node, and the mission will end.

NOTE

Omega is Hotkeyed to F9 for this mission. Tapping F9 will target the two transports. Once the transports are targeted, pressing "G" will target the unit (or one of the units) targeting the transports. Once you have this information, order someone to destroy the offending Shivan.

MISSION: BLACK OMEGA

PRIMARY OBJECTIVES

✦ Escort Omega to Jump Node

SECONDARY OBJECTIVES

✦ Destroy the Anvil

ENEMY FORCES

Aries Wing:	**12 PVF Thoth (4 Flights of 3 Craft)**
Virgo Wing:	**12 PVF Horus (4 Flights of 3 Craft)**
Leo Wing:	**4 PVB Osiris (2 Flights of 2 Craft)**
Anvil:	**PVD Typhon**

FRIENDLY FORCES

Alpha Wing:	**4 GTB Ursa**
Beta Wing:	**4 GTF Ulysses**
Gamma Wing:	**4 GTF Hercules**

WINNING

NOTE

By coordinating with your wingmates, you can swamp the destroyer with the Harbringers. This can seriously weaken her. Then call for a reload.

The last in the series of single player ports. Although this is a tad bit tougher than its single player counterpart, it is not unwinnable. The Hammer of Light fighter/bomber contingent is 33% stronger, but then you are flying with real wingmen. I think it's an even tradeoff.

As in the single mission, tell the Beta Ulysses to down the Leo wing bombers, form Gamma on your wing, order Alpha to attack the Anvil, and head in with them.

Continue hounding the Anvil while Beta —fresh from extinguishing the Vasudan bomber's flames— protects Omega 2. Even if you lose Omega 1 before the Vasudan bombers are destroyed, you can still win the scenario as long as Omega 2 lives.

Pound the Anvil until she blows. Even if you fail to destroy the Anvil before Omega 2 flies by, she may be too busy with your attack to worry about her. Once the Anvil is destroyed and whatever Omegas survive have departed, the mission will end.

NOTE

Take the default craft; they are a good selection. If you are flying an Ursa, load it with 4 Harbringers, 10 Phoenix and twin Prometheus. The Phoenix and Prometheus are for taking out laser/missile turrets. The Harbringers are for taking out your ship. Don't worry about dogfighting. If you are flying an Ursa, you are not going to be dogfighting.

NOTE

There are 28 Vasudan Fighters in this battle. Not an incredible number by multiplayer standards. However, you may find that attacking one of the Vasudan fighter wings (Virgo or Aries) not only takes the weight off Alpha, but aids in protecting the Omega twins.

THE LAST HOPE

The Hope is the most beloved destroyer of the Vasudan people. In the final days of the Shivan war it and its crew performed its most amazing operations. This is the story of those operations. This is the last story of Vasuda prime.

MISSION: EXODUS

NOTE

Be advised that bombs can be targeted and shot down. If you are having trouble destroying the Anvil with the headlong rush described above, try taking out some, if not all, of its weapons systems before you rain the bombs.

PRIMARY OBJECTIVES

✦ Protect Allied ships

✦ Secure area until relief arrives

ENEMY FORCES

Asura Wing:	**6 SB Nephilim, 3 SF Basilisk (3 Flights of 2 Nephilim and 1 Basilisk)**
Arjuna Wing:	**8 SF Basilisk (2 Flights of 4 Craft)**
Bheema Wing:	**12 SF Basilisk (3 Flights of 4 Craft)**
Indra Wing:	**6 SB Shaitan (3 Flights of 2 Craft)**
Kali Wing:	**4 SB Shaitan (2 Flights of 2 Craft)**
Krishna Wing:	**9 SF Scorpion (3 Flights of 3 Craft)**
Rama Wing:	**2 SF Basilisk, 3 SB Nephilim**
Cain:	**PVC Lilith**
Able:	**PVC Lilith**

FRIENDLY FORCES

Alpha Wing:	**4 PVF Seth**
Epsilon Wing:	**4 GTF Hercules**
Phi Wing:	**2 PVF Anubis, 2 PVF Seth, 3 PVF Horus**
Theta Wing:	**3 GTFR Poseidon**
Zeta Wing:	**4 GTF Hercules**
Kappa Wing:	**6 PVFR Satis, 1 PVFR Bast, 3 PVFR Ma'at**
Mu Wing:	**3 PVT Isis**
Pi Wing:	**4 PVF Horus**
Rho Wing:	**2 PVF Anubis**
VC 3 16:	**VC3 Cargo Pod**
VAC 4 17:	**VC4 Cargo Pod**

NOTE

Beware, there are many more Shivan craft in this multiplayer version. This is no time to dilly-dally. You must strike fast and hard.

WINNING

This mission is the multiplayer version of Act III, Mission 1. As such, the strategy is nearly identical. You get to fly Vasudan fighters, and that's nice. I'd take a Thoth and arm it with Hornets and Banshee lasers. You may want to give your wingmates something a tad heavier, perhaps the default Seths, for example.

The Shivan bombers are bad news for the transports, so concentrate on them. The first Shivan bombers to take aim at the Vasudan transports are Indra and Kali wings. There are ten in all.

They are, however, no match for your nimble Thoth. At this point in the mission, you can keep the Vasudans safe by aggressively attacking the Shivans.

Once Mu Wing enters, direct PHI to protect them while you and your friends from Alpha/Epsilon concentrate on the newly arrived fighters and bombers from Arjuna wings. Destroy these aliens, and it's all downhill from here.

The cruisers are not as big a problem as they would initially seem. You have the numbers to swamp them with firepower. Do so. Once they are knocked out, little stands between yourself and victory.

MISSION: LAST HOPE

PRIMARY OBJECTIVES

✦ Protect the Hope

ENEMY FORCES

Indra Wing:	12 SB Nephilim (3 Flights of 4 Craft)
Asura Wing:	4 SB Nephilim (2 Flights of 2 Craft)
Bheema Wing:	3 SB Shaitan
Krishna Wing:	3 SF Manticore
Arjuna Wing:	3 SF Dragon
Vishnu Wing:	3 SF Manticore
Durga Wing:	4 SF Dragon
Kali Wing:	12 SB Nephilim (2 Flights of 6 Craft)
Rama Wing:	9 SF Scorpions (3 Flights of 3 Craft)

FRIENDLY FORCES

Alpha Wing:	4 PVF Seth
Theta Wing:	4 GTF Ulysses
Mu Wing:	4 PVF Thoth
Rho Wing:	4 PVF Thoth
Hope:	PVD Typhon
Macross:	PVC Aten
Isis Repair:	PVT Isis

WINNING

Again, a multiplayer scenario based on the single player scenario of a similar ilk. Unfortunately in this version, the computer gets more stuff, and you get less. No matter, it's still time to kick some Shivan butt. Grab a Thoth, put the rest of Alpha in Seths—they need the firepower to take out the Thunder. If you're a bomber kind of pilot, you may want to take a Seth also.

As beforehand toward the Antares jump node with your wingmates in tow. The Hope will jump in and shortly thereafter its pursuers arrive.

About the time that the first three Vasudan freighters (Kappa 4-6) exit, the Vasudans of Rho and PHI wings will begin trickling in. These folks will guard the Vasudans transiting between the jumps nodes but are otherwise worthless. You can, however, direct them to protect freighters or even assist your attacks. But with a couple of good human wingmates in Alpha, you shouldn't need them to down fighters. Just have them guard freighters and pose as laser fodder.

NOTE

The closer you are to the Antares jump node when the Hope arrives, the sooner you can destroy the bombers of Indra wing. Your goal is to take out this wing of bombers before they can damage the Hope.

The Indra and Asura waves arrive in quick succession after you destroy the first Shivan bombers. You may want to designate the Terran wing, Theta, to guard the Hope while you and your human friends devastate the Shivan bomber.

As you're working on these Shivans, Arjuna, Bheema, and Krishna arrive. Put two Alphans on the Arjuna Dragons, and attack the bombers of Bheema with everyone else. After the Shaitans and Dragon are vaporized, mop up the Manticores.

Just like the single player mission, the Cain class Shivan cruiser arrives, as does the Isis repair ship. Order all hands to bombard the Lightning. Once the Lightning goes down, another Cain class, the Thunder, arrives. At least the Vasudan cruiser Aten zips in to help you take this one down. Destroy it (the Shivan, NOT the Vasudan) as you did the first.

Unfortunately, your trials are not over yet. Durga Wing, comprising four Dragons and Vishnu with six Manticore, enter, and by the time they're destroyed, you'll probably be down a couple of fighters.

The Shivans are nothing if not persistent, and in a final effort, they throw Kali and Rama wing at you and your pals. Splash them, wait for the Vasudan Mu and Rho wings to arrive, and the mission ends.

NOTE

After the Lightning goes down, you'll have a short breather before the Thunder appears. It's a good idea to rearm (Shift+R).

MISSION:

A FAILURE TO COMMUNICATE

PRIMARY OBJECTIVES

✦ Protect Aquilae installation

ENEMY FORCES

Arjuna Wing:	24 SF Manticore (6 Flights of 4 Craft)
Asura Wing:	4 SB Shaitan
Bheema Wing:	24 SB Nephilim (6 flights of 4 Craft)
Deva Wing:	4 SF Dragon
Karna Wing:	4 SF Basilisk
Krishna Wing:	6 SF Basilisk
Rama Wing:	3 SF Scorpions
Lucifer	

FRIENDLY FORCES

Alpha Wing:	4 PVF Horus
Cancer Wing:	4 PVF Thoth
Hope:	PVD Typhon
Aquilae Communications:	GTSC Faustus

WINNING

Like its single player counterpart (Act III, Mission 3), this mission opens with the destruction of the Aquilae. Don't let it get you down, there is still plenty of work to be done. And hey, at least you get to fly one of those neat Vasudan Horus fighters.

To win, you must escort the Aquilae installation escape pods. You can do this by killing Shivans quicker than they kill the pods. Use Cancer and Alpha to attack Shivan Deva wing. Move quickly—you have about two minutes to knock them out before more trouble arrives.

Once you vaporize these two wings, Krishna arrives. As if that is not enough bad news, Asura and Rama pop up shortly thereafter. Attack Krishna with Cancer while you fly with Alpha against Asura and Rama.

Return to the Communications station and wait for Bheema and Arjuna to arrive. Fly out to meet them, and defeat them. Unlike the single player version of the scenario, there are six waves of bombers and fighters to work through here. Once you do, however, the mission will end.

NOTE

Whenever possible, engage the enemy within weapon range of the Hope. She'll destroy a lot of your adversaries for you.

MISSION: LEVIATHAN DUEL

PRIMARY OBJECTIVES

✦ **Player One:** Protect Zaldhun (Bonus: Destroy Arcticon)

✦ **Player Two:** Protect Arcticon (Bonus: Destroy Zaldhun)

PLAYER ONE FORCES

Zeta Wing:	2 GTF Ulysses, 2 GTB Medusas
Omicron Wing:	8 GTF Hercules (4 Flights of 2 Craft)
Zaldhun:	GTC Leviathan

PLAYER TWO FORCES

Alpha Wing:	2 GTF Ulysses, 2 GTB Medusas
Theta Wing:	8 GTF Hercules (4 Flights of 2 Craft)
Arcticon:	GTC

WINNING

Kind of like a game of chess, but more fun. The job is simple —kill the enemy cruiser (forget what the objectives say, it's way more fun to just kill the enemy cruiser).

Order your AI fighters (Omicron and Theta wings) to guard their respective cruisers. If you forget, don't worry, that is their default mode and their arrival anchor.

The "real" (Alpha and Zeta) pilots should saddle up their Ulysses and Medusas and head for the enemy cruiser. The fighter jocks should try to pull the cruiser's guardians away from the ship before

NOTE

This mission is all about staying unpredictable. If you fly it the same way every time, you are going to lose. For a change, try sending everyone (including the AI fighters) against the enemy cruiser. You may swamp its defenses and bring it down quickly. Alternatively, set the respawn for one or two, and guard your own cruiser with everyone (including the "real" pilots). When the enemy comes calling you can jump him, and quickly take out all his bombers.

engaging. The bombers should take out the cruiser's weapon systems first. The fighter pilots should be ready to peel off at the first sign of trouble and attack any craft attacking the bombers.

Once everyone has dumped their secondary ordnance, call for a resupply (Shift + R). The fighters should stand watch while the bombers resupply, then take their own turns.

After resupply, head back in and do some more damage. If the cruiser is hurting (30%), don't resupply again. Stay close and finish her off with your primary weapons. Once she reaches the critical level, she will flee.

MISSION: CLOSING THE GATE

PRIMARY OBJECTIVES

✦ **GTA Objective:** Destroy PVD Gate

✦ **Vasudan Objective:** Protect PVD Gate

GTA FORCES

Alpha Wing: **4 GTF Ulysses**
Tornado: **GTC Fenris**

VASUDAN FORCES

Epsilon Wing: **150 PVF Seth (50 Flights of 3 Craft)**
Zeta Wing: **4 PVF Thoth**
Gate: **PVC Aten**

WINNING

This is certainly not the mission for rookie Terran pilots. You must not only face a similar number of human piloted Thoths, you have a undamable trickle of AI piloted Seths nipping at your flanks.

It is best for the more experienced pilots to fly for the honor of the Terrans, while those in the shallow end of the experience or talent matrix fly for the grand Vasudan navy.

The Terrans should pump up their shields (the Home key) and blast in on the Vasudans. The Herc pilots need sow as much laser-light laced trouble as possible. Focus on the Thoths —they are the human —and supposedly better— pilots. Meanwhile back at the Tsunami ranch, the Athenas commence their bombing runs. As always, concentrate on the weapon systems first, and destroy all the systems in one area if possible. Do so, and you won't have to weather the capital ship's fire as you shred her armor.

NOTE

Ditch the default Ulysses. You have at a lot of pounding to do, and the Ulysses are not the right sticks for the job. I like a two Herc/two Athena combo. The Hercs can fly against other fighters, yet still pack quite a wallop on their bombing runs. Conversely, the Athena is a good (albeit a bit light) bomber yet , in the right hands, can hold its own in a dogfight.

NOTE

Be advised, the Tornado will try to help you in your quest for glory. Her in-mission AI is set to "Chase Gate." That means she will try to track down and engage the Vasudan cruiser.

The Vasudan pilots should try to engage the Terrans within a thousand meters of the Gate. By doing so, the Gate will be able to lend her awesome power to your attacks.

Keep an eye on the Tornado. If the Gate takes heavy damage, target her and press "G" to reveal her assailants. If the Tornado is lasing her, send some Epsilon folks after the Tornado. I doubt they will bring her down, but they will distract her.

MISSION: CLASH

PRIMARY OBJECTIVES

✦ **GTA:**   Destroy Predator and Ghost

✦ **Vasudan:**   *Destroy Havoc and Piranha*

GTA FORCES

Alpha Wing:	*4 GTF Ulysses*
Delta Wing:	*20 GTB Ursas (5 Flights of 4 Craft)*
Havoc:	*GTC Leviathan*
Piranha:	*GTC Fenris*

VASUDAN FORCES

Zeta Wing:	*4 PVF Thoth*
Omicron Wing:	*20 PVB Amun*
Predator:	*PVC Aten*
Ghost:	*PVC Aten*

WINNING

This is a straight up brawl if there ever was one. A refreshing change from some of the other multi-player mega-missions, you can usually fly this one in under 15 minutes.

The goals and equipment for both sides are nearly identical. Heck, the Ulysses even looks a little like the Thoth. Because of the mirrored approach to this scenario, the strategies remain the same, whether you are Terran or Vasudan.

Sic your bombers —be they Ursas or Amun— on the closest capital ship. These are dumb AI types, so you just have to hope that their numbers (20) can tip the scales.

Meanwhile concentrate on taking out the enemy fighters. These are piloted by real life forms and, if left to their own devices, will annihilate your bombers. Each player can have up to 50 respawns (depending on host settings), so this might take awhile. If you can gain the upper hand, split a couple of fighters off to engage the enemy bombers. Once you can do that, it won't be long until the enemy is bomberless.

After you gain the upper hand in bombers, that —coupled with your own capital ship weapon systems— should soon destroy the enemy.

MISSION: GUARD DUTY

PRIMARY OBJECTIVES

✦ **GTA Objective:**   Protect the El Dorado

✦ **Vasudan Objective:** Destroy The El Dorado

GTA FORCES

Alpha Wing:	4 GTF Ulysses
Delta Wing:	100 GTF Valkyrie (50 Flights of 2 Craft)
Iota Wing:	100 GTF Valkyrie (50 Flights of 2 Craft)
El Dorado:	GTI Arcadia

VASUDAN FORCES

Omega Wing:	20 PVB Amum (10 Flights of 2 Craft)
Zeta Wing:	4 PVF Thoth

WINNING

> **NOTE**
>
> *The El Dorado is no cruiser, but she is not to be taken lightly. 24 laser turrets dot the station's hull. That's a lot of energetic destruction for the unwary.*

> **NOTE**
>
> *As always, try to engage the Terran fighters out of the El Dorado weapons range. You'll live much longer.*

In many ways this mission is the mirror image of "Closing the Gate." The offensive shoe is on the other foot, claw, or whatever Vasudans have. While the El Dorado is not nearly as tough as the Aten class cruiser the Terrans destroyed in the aforementioned scenario, the Terran have a swarm of fighters the Vasudans must wade through to win.

As the Vasudan, your *raison d'être* is simple: massacre Terran fighters. Omega wing has 20 bombers, no more, no less. If the El Dorado isn't space waste by the time your last PVB Amum goes down, you'll never win the scenario. The Ulysses of the Terran Alpha wing are the priority. These are piloted by humans and pose the greatest threat to your bombers.

When and if you down the human Terrans, you can pounce on Delta and Iota or even lend a hand with the El Dorado. Either way, you're halfway home once the carbon based life form pilots are out of the picture.

The Terran's job is equally simple: kill Vasudan bombers. Please note that to kill Vasudan bombers, you must be alive and kicking, flying, or whatever. This means that at least half of Alpha wing will need to engage Zeta wing while the other two attack Omega's bombers. You can order your AI fighters to engage the Vasudan fighters, bombers, or just tell them to guard the El Dorado. I prefer the guard El Dorado route.

> **NOTE**
>
> *Although there are more fighters in Delta and Iota wings than you care to think of, each wave only has two. So, they trickle in. They will always be there, but they are not an overwhelming force.*

> **NOTE**
>
> *For a change of pace, give two Zeta wing pilots PVB Osiris bombers. These pilots will be responsible for taking out as many El Doradan lasers as they can. This really opens the way for your AI bombers. Unfortunately, the two remaining Vasudan fighter pilots have to be damn good to avoid being shot to pieces.*

MISSION: BASTION OF LIGHT

PRIMARY OBJECTIVES

✦ GTA: Protect the GTI Fortress

✦ Hammer of Light: Destroy the GTI Fortress

GTA FORCES

Aries Wing:	4 X PVF Horus
Alpha Wing:	4 X GTF Ulysses
Beta Wing:	4 X GTF Hercules
Bastion:	GTD Orion
Fortress:	GTI Arcadia

HAMMER OF LIGHT FORCES

Omicron Wing:	2 PVF Horus
Theta Wing:	4 PVF Thoth
Zeta:	4 X PVB Amun
Cleopatra:	PVC Aten
Pharoah:	PVC Aten
Ramses:	PVC Aten
Scarab:	PVC Aten

> **NOTE**
>
> The Bastion is way more powerful than any one PVC Aten class cruiser. But of course there is more than one. It will be hurt during its attack, your job is to limit that damage. If the Bastion's hull drops to 25%, she will warp out.

> **NOTE**
>
> If things are going well, assign Beta wing to protect the Bastion. Or, if things are going very well, the Fortress. With Beta's Hercs orbiting their charge, take Alpha and attack whatever cruiser the Bastion is currently targeting.

WINNING

As the Terran, you must try to protect the Fortress until the Bastion arrives. Failing that, protect the seven pods the Fortress will spew as she dies. Once the Bastion enters, it will go for the Hammer of Light cruisers. Let it do its work, while you keep the HOL fighters and bombers off its back.

The Hammer of Light player needs to move fast. Take down the Fortress before the Bastion arrives, or you may never take it down. Once the Fortress is out of the way, mass your cruiser strength and hope it will be enough to take out the Bastion when it arrives.

MISSION: VASUDAN GAUNTLET MULTI-4

PRIMARY OBJECTIVES

✦ Destroy all ships in the Gauntlet.

SECONDARY OBJECTIVES

✦ Destroy intermediate phases.

ENEMY FORCES

Anubis 1:	3 PVF Anubis
Anubis B:	5 PVF Anubis
Seth A:	3 PVF Seth
Anubis C:	6 PVF Anubis
Seth B:	4 PVF Seth (2 Flights of 2 Craft)
Horus A:	4 PVF Horus (GTS Centaur)
Horus B:	12 PVF Horus (2 Flights of 6 Craft)
Seth C:	10 PVF Seth (2 Flights of 5 Craft)
Thoth A:	8 PVF Thoth (2 Flights of 4 Craft)
Thoth B:	12 PVF Thoth (3 Flights of 4 Craft)
Thoth C:	12 PVF Thoth (3 Flights of 4 Craft)
Anubis D	12 PVF Thoth (3 Flights of 4 Craft) GTS Centaur
Seth D:	12 PVF Seth (3 Flights of 4 Craft) Anubis D
Horus C:	24 PVF Horus (4 Flights of 6 Craft) Seth D
Thoth D:	24 PVF Thoth (4 Flights of 6 Craft) Horus C
Thoth E:	198 PVF Thoth (99 Flights of 2 Craft)
Thoth F:	297 PVF Thoth (99 Flights of 3 Craft)
Abydos:	PVC Aten
Khufu:	PVD
Isis	

WINNING

> **NOTE**
>
> The Destruction of Seth B satisfies the secondary objectives.

Well, as Bert Jones used to say, "There ain't nothing to it, but to do it." Report to the stable, check out your favorite ride, and jump in.

I like a Herc. Compared to the nimble Vasudan fighters, it's a plodder. But it only takes a couple of shots from its twin Banshees to down an Anuban. On top of that, it carries 120 Hornets. Believe me, you'll need them.

The Vasudan wings are listed in their order of appearance. In general, the destruction of each wing is the cue for the arrival of the next. After Seth B is destroyed, GTA Command will send in rearming ships. Unfortunately, Horus A, which also enters after Seth B is destroyed, will attempt to knock out the ships. A couple of Fighters should keep the Horans occupied while the others rearm. Once you are rearmed, fight Horans and give the others a chance to stock up on missiles.

> **NOTE**
>
> A PVT Isis also enters here. Take her out first. It's a good warm-up for the cruiser.

> **NOTE**
>
> Uh, although there is now a backlog of Thoths waiting to get at you, if you don't kill the first, no more will come. Of course, if you don't kill the first, he may kill you—but life is full of compromises.

Keep shooting. After you destroy Thoth C, Phase 2 is complete and more reload ships will enter. Protect them, reload, and continue. Once Thoth D is destroyed, Phase 3 is complete.

Once Thoth D is destroyed, more rearm ships appear, as does the PVC Abydos. This bad boy brings in Thoth E. This wing represents a virtually unlimited supply of fighters.

If you have real, living wingmates, they may still be alive. Any regenerated AI may still be there to help you, too. Either way, put everything into taking out the Abydos. Once it is gone, so are its fighters, and Phase 4 is complete.

The bad news is a Typhoon class destroyer, The Khufu now enters. With her comes the fighters of Thoth F. Destroy them both, and you win. Now, wasn't that easy?

MISSION: SHIVAN GAUNTLET MULTI-4

PRIMARY OBJECTIVES

✦ Destory all ships in the gauntlet.

SECONDARY OBJECTIVES

✦ Destroy intermediate phases.

ENEMY FORCES

Basilisk A:	3 SF Basilisk
Basilisk B:	5 SF Basilisk
Scorpion A:	3 SF Scorpion
Basilisk C:	6 SF Basilisk
Scorpion B:	4 Scorpion (2 Flights of 2 Craft)
Manticore A:	4 SF Manticore
Manticore B:	12 SF Manticore (2 Flights of 6 Craft)
Scorpion C:	10 SF Scorpion (2 Flights of 5 Craft)
Dragon A:	8 SF Dragon (2 Flights of 4 Craft)
Dragon B:	12 SF Dragon (3 Flights of 4 Craft)
Dragon C:	12 SF Dragon (3 Flights of 4 Craft)
Basilisk D:	12 SF Basilisk (3 Flights of 4 Craft)
Scorpion D:	12 SF Scorpion (3 Flights of 4 Craft)
Manticore C:	24 SF Manticore (4 Flights of 6 Craft)
Dragon D:	24 SF Dragons (4 Flights of 6 Craft)
Dragon E:	188 SF Dragons (99 Flights of 2 Craft)
Dragon F:	188 SF Dragons (99 Flights of 2 Craft)
Abaddon:	SC Cain
Sheol:	SD DEmon

FRIENDLY FORCES

Alpha Wing:	2 GTF Ulysses
Beta Wing:	1 GTF Ulysses
Gamma Wing:	1 GTF Ulysses

WINNING

Well, what can you say? The three Gauntlet missions (Vasudan, Shivan, and Terran) are nearly identical. Only the equipment differs. How much it differs in the Shivan Gauntlet, however, is bad news for the Terran pilots. You can handle the Shivan fighters. They are good, but you can handle them. The real fly in the galactic ointment is the Demon class destroyer, Sheol. After destroying hundreds of fighters and the SC Abaddon cruiser, she will be a tough nut to crack.

I'd take two Ulysses and two Hercs for this mission. The Hercs lack the Ulysses dartiness, but carry a heavier weapons load. That load will come in handy when attacking the Sheol. But first you have to get there...

The tactics are simple: fly your butt off. The Shivan wings come in the order listed above. With a couple of exceptions, Destroying one wing triggers the next. Manticore A, Basilisk D, and Dragon E, enter when the GTA command calls in Centaur 1, 4, and 7, respectively. Of course the Dragon E waves stop when the Abaddon is destroyed. Damage to the Sheol's weapon systems trigger Dragon F's entrance.

MISSION: TERRAN GAUNTLET MULTI-4

PRIMARY OBJECTIVES

✦ Destroy all ships in the gauntlet

SECONDARY OBJECTIVES

✦ Destroy intermediate phases.

ENEMY FORCES

Apollo A:	1 GTF Apollo
Apollo B:	5 GTF Apollo
Valkyrie A:	3 GTF Valkyrie
Apollo C:	6 GTF Apollo
Valkyrie B:	4 GTF Valkyrie (2 Flights of 2 Craft)
Hercules A:	4 GTF Hercules
Hercules B:	12 GTF Hercules (2 Flights of 6 Craft)
Valkyrie C:	10 GTF Valkyrie (2 Flights of 5 Craft)
Ulysses A:	8 GTF Ulysses (2 Flights of 4 Craft)
Ulysses B:	12 GTF Ulysses (3 Flights of 4 Craft)
Ulysses C:	12 GTF Ulysses (3 Flights of 4 Craft)
Apollo D:	12 GTF Apollo (3 Flights of 4 Craft)
Valkyrie D:	12 GTF Valkyrie (3 Flights of 4 Craft)
Hercules C:	24 GTF Hercules (4 Flights of Craft)
Ulysses D:	24 GTF Ulysses (4 Flights of 6 Craft)
Ulysses E:	188 GTF Ulysses (99 Flights of 2 Craft)
Ulysses F:	188 GTF Ulysses (99 Flights of 2 craft)
Rickover:	GTC Levathan
Nietzsche:	GTD Orion

FRIENDLY FORCES

Alpha Wing:	2 GTF Ulysses
Beta Wing:	1 GTF Ulyssses
Gamma Wing:	1 GTF Ulysses

WINNING

Another of the challenging "Gauntlet" missions. I think this is the easiest. Terran space superiority fighters are a tad less maneuverable than their alien counterparts. So, you don't need nimble craft to bring them down (the Ulysses is the exception -but a good human can outfly a computer driven Ulysses any day.)Accordingly, outfit all four pilots with Hercules. By doing so, you'll have the punch to take out the mission ending cruiser and destroyer.

As with the other guantlets, the trick is too fly hard and kill lots of enemies. If you do you'll win.

> **NOTE**
>
> If you find the rebel fighter too tough to tame with Hercs try either adjusting the mission difficulty or taking Ulysses.

MISSION: CONVOY ASSAULT

PRIMARY OBJECTIVES

✦ Destroy the Convoy

ENEMY FORCES

Aries Wing:	*6 PVF Horus*
Pisces Wing:	*3 PVF Seth*
PVT Johnson:	*PVT Isis*
PVT Quest:	*PVT Isis*
PVT Star:	*PVT Isis*
PVT McPherson:	*PVT Isis*
PVFR Flame:	*PVFR Ma'at*
PVFR Nova:	*PVFR Ma'at*
PVFR Bay:	*PVFR Satis*
PVFR System:	*PVFR Satis*

FRIENDLY FORCES

Alpha Wing:	*4 GTF Ulysses*

WINNING

Okay folks, the clock is ticking and you have about eight minutes to destroy the convoy. If you are playing ships/weapons free, here is what I'd take: Two pilots drive Medusas loaded with Tsunami, Phoenix, and a Prometheus. The other two stick jockeys should fly Ulysses.

The pilots in the Ulysses should engage the Vasudan fighters. You must keep them off the bombers' butts. Meanwhile, back at the bombing ranch, the Medusas pick off the transports and freighters.

The bomber pilots need to be frugal with the weapons. Use Phoenix missiles to soften up the freighters'/transports' laser turrets from afar, finish the job with the Prometheus, then take out the vessel with a Tsunami. One bomber pilot should use his Tsunamis on the freighters, the other on the transports.

Obviously, the Ulysses pilots should take out the Vasudan fighters. When and if that's done, they can help with the remaining Vasudan freighter/transports.

MISSION: ORION RECOVERY

PRIMARY OBJECTIVES

✦ Recover the Storm

ENEMY FORCES

Arjuna Wing:	6 SF Basilisk
Krishna Wing:	4 SF Manticore
Rama Wing:	4 SF Manticore
Vishnu Wing:	5 SF Basilisk
Minotaur:	ST Azreal

FRIENDLY FORCES

Alpha Wing:	4 GTF Ulysses
Storm:	GTD Orion
Source:	GTT Elysium

WINNING

NOTE

The difficulty of this mission ties strongly to the difficulty level you have set. At medium and above, this is a tough nut to crack. Below medium, it is much more manageable.

This mission is simple in concept, yet can be difficult in execution. All you have to do is keep the 19 Shivan fighters off the backs of the Storm and the Source (especially the Source), and destroy the Minotaur when it arrives. Problem is, those 19 Shivan fighters can be a real pain in the thruster.

Spend the mission's opening moments slamming the Shivans of Arjuna and Krishna wing. Two Ulysses should guard the Source when it enters. The other two should keep on wasting Shivans.

As soon as Rama wing and the Minotaur arrive, one of the fighter killers should peal off and take out the Minotaur while the other covers. When the Source docks, all four Terran pilots should once again lay into the Shivan fighters. If you maintain the upper hand, the Source will finish her repairs, GTA Command will announce that it is sending tugs and fighters to bring the Storm home, and the mission will end.

MISSION: CRUISER RESCUE

PRIMARY OBJECTIVES

✦ Rescue the Cruiser

ENEMY FORCES

Arjuna Wing:	6 SF Manticore
Krishna Wing:	300 SF Manticore (50 Fights of 6 Craft)
Rama Wing:	2 SF Basilisk

FRIENDLY FORCES

Alpha Wing:	2 GTF Ulysses
Orb:	GTC Leviathan

WINNING

If you love to dogfight. I mean REALLY LOVE to dogfight, this is the mission for you. Nothing subtle here; just massacre Shivans.

The bad guys will never stop coming. The trick is to take them out quickly. If you muck around, they are going to bring down the Orb. Make sure you have auto target on and wade into the battle. Let your wingmate do his own thing. Remember; the more Shivans you occupy, the fewer Shivans that attack the Orb.

About five minutes into the mission, support one arrives. Five minutes later, the Orb is ready to roll, and she departs (without even saying thank you). Her departure signals your victory.

MISSION: UNSTOPPABLE

PRIMARY OBJECTIVES

✦ Destroy the Hellfire

ENEMY FORCES

Arjuna Wing:	6 SF Basilisk
Bheema Wing:	600 SF Basilisk (100 Flights of 6 Craft)
Indra Wing:	24 SF Manticore (6 Flights of 4 Craft)
Krishna Wing:	600 SF Basilisk (100 Flights of 6 Craft)
Rama Wing:	600 SF Basilisk (100 Flights of 6 Craft)
Hellfire:	SD Demon

FRIENDLY FORCES

Alpha Wing:	4 GTF Ulysses
Beta Wing:	2 GTB Ursa
Iota Wing:	3 GTF Apollo
Hoyle:	GTSC Faustus
Omen:	GTSC Omen
Hoplit:	GTC Fenris

WINNING

Whoever flies in Beta wing should stick with the Ursas. Humans in Alpha may want to take Hercs—they can handle the fighters, yet have the punch to stick it to the Hellfire. AI Alphas should stick with Ulysses and be used as fighter cover.

Send Iota against Arjuna as soon as the mission opens. They will get creamed, but they may take a couple with them. If Alpha has carbon-based pilots, send two against the Krishna fighters while the other two join Beta in attacking the Hellfire.

> **NOTE**
>
> This is a good mission to try out the latest in Vasudan hardware. The PVF Thoth is a good fighter—nimble, yet well armed. Equip both yourself and your wingmate with one. It's great for dodging laser bolts and keeping you alive. On top of that, the Manticores can't shake them off their tales.

> **NOTE**
>
> The Orb is no wussy. Her lasers can take down their share of Shivans. Whenever possible, fight within her laser range. You'll be surprised how many of your prey she downs.

> **NOTE**
>
> Don't be intimidated by the large number of Shivan ships in the order of battle. They trickle in waves of six. You'll never see 1800 Shivan fighters at once. You'd be dead long before that, so cheer up.

> **NOTE**
>
> Don't count on the Hoplite for much help. She is grievously wounded and will blow within a couple of minutes after the mission opens.

As the note says, concentrate on the Hellfire's engines. To do that, however, you will probably need to knock out a few of its laser turrets first. Concentrate on thinning the destroyer's defenses, and then knock out its engines.

There are no Shivan bombers, and most the of the fighters just want to protect the Hellfire. In other words, if you keep the destroyer away from the science stations, the battle is nearly won.

Once the engines are destroyed, take out enough weapon systems to create a blind spot from which you can bombard the Hellfire until she blows.

MISSION: VASUDAN ASSAULT

PRIMARY OBJECTIVES

✦ Destroy the PVD Ptolemy

✦ Destroy PVC Gateway

ENEMY FORCES

Aries Wing:	600 PVF Thoth (100 Flights of 6 Craft)
Capricorn Wing:	300 PVF Thoth, 200 PVF Seth, 100 PVF Horus (100 Flights of 3 Thoth, 2 Seth, and 1 Horus)
Cancer Wing:	600 PVF Thoth (100 Flights of 6 Craft)
Gemini Wing:	200 PVF Thoth, 200 PVF Seth, 200 PVF Anubis (100 Flights of 2 Thoth, 2 Seth, 2 Anubis)
Pisces Wing:	6 PVF Horus
Virgo Wing:	12 PVF Horus (3 Flights of 4 Craft)
Gateway:	PVC Aten
Ptolemy:	PVD Typhoon

FRIENDLY FORCES

Alpha Wing:	4 GTF Ulysses
Beta Wing:	4 GTF Ursa

WINNING

There are 2418 fighters in this mission. Count 'em. You have eight. Well, actually four and four bombers. That's the bad news. There are, however, two bits of good news: First, you don't *have to* kill a single enemy fighter to win. Second, all 2418 don't come at you at once.

In short, you will never win by eliminating the enemy fighters and then attacking the capital ships. To win this one, you must keep the fighters at bay while attacking first the Ptolamy and then the Gateway.

NOTE

There are two ways to fly cover: You can wade into any and every Vasudan fighter, or you can stick close by Beta wing, attacking anything that threatens them.
I prefer to wade in. If you use this approach, try to wade into the fighters currently targeting the bombers. Target a Beta craft, then press "G" to locate its tormentor.

Beta pilots should attack the destroyer first. Keep Alpha in the Ulysses. Arm them with Prometheus and Hornets, and fly cover for Beta.

You bomber pilots should attack the Ptolemy from the side, facing away from the Gateway. This reduces your incoming fire. Take out all the weapons systems on that side, then strafe the monster until it goes down.

Once the Ptolemy goes down, rearm and switch your attention to the Gateway. Use the same tactics, and it to will soon explode.

NOTE

Bomber pilots should resist the urge to hang in one place while lighting up the capital ships. This makes them an easy target for Vasudan pilots. Cruise down the length of the ship as you fire your weapons.

INDEX

T